THE SCANDAL OF THE KINGDOM

WORKBOOK

HOW THE **PARABLES OF JESUS** REVOLUTIONIZE LIFE WITH GOD

BASED ON THE BOOK BY

DALLAS WILLARD

WRITTEN BY JAN JOHNSON

The Scandal of the Kingdom Workbook

Published in Grand Rapids, Michigan, by HarperChristian Resources. HarperChristian Resources is a registered trademark of HarperCollins Christian Publishing, Inc.

Requests for information should be sent to customercare@harpercollins.com.

ISBN 978-0-310-17035-8 (softcover)
ISBN 978-0-310-17036-5 (ebook)

HarperChristian Resources titles may be purchased in bulk for church, business, fundraising, or ministry use. For information, please email ResourceSpecialist@ChurchSource.com.

First Printing September 2024 / Printed in the United States of America

CONTENTS

INTRODUCTION

If you've read stories to children, you know that a lot happens behind their eyes and in their minds besides simply hearing words. You can see it on their faces—they're having an *experience*! They perk up if one of the characters is like them. They feel sad when the characters have troubles. The same is true for us adults with certain books and movies.

Jesus knew the power of narrative, so he offered stories to illustrate truths about God and his kingdom. Stories often work better than trying to follow outlined theories or cause-and-effect dynamics. Truths that can be explained in a sentence or two are easily forgotten. Other truths are difficult to "put on," to really become a part of our lives, to be *realized*, because we can't picture them. To understand, remember, and realize truth—to taste it, see it, smell it—is a different thing. This is what Jesus wanted for us: to absorb truth as fully as possible.

This is the goal of *The Scandal of the Kingdom Workbook*—to help you explore and experience the truths from Dallas Willard's book. It has been said that people don't really learn from experience but from *reflecting on experience*. Using this workbook will set the table for you to sit down, feast on that experience, and consider what it means to you. In that process, you are likely to hear God. So, some exercises ask you to pause and reflect—please don't skip them. If you do, you will miss out on some high-end opportunities to hear God.

If you haven't yet read *The Scandal of the Kingdom*, you will still be fine using the workbook. It was designed to stand alone. It shares the book's outline, central ideas, and some of its text, but practical ideas have been added as well as questions, reminders of key terms, and suggestions for further reading. If you have read the book, using the workbook will give you some added insight to ponder and added time to reflect—to experience Jesus.

— JAN JOHNSON

HOW TO USE THIS WORKBOOK

This workbook may be used by individuals or groups. If you use it as an individual, please don't approach it with the mindset of "getting through" the content. Go at the pace that Jesus takes you. Often, a passage you read the day before or last week will continue to resonate with you. You may even wake in the middle of the night thinking about it. Don't ignore this! Get out your workbook and scribble more notes in it. Then enter into a conversation with God about it.

If you're using this workbook in a group setting, pay attention to the answers that other people give. Group learning will allow Jesus to speak to you through other people—even those in the group who annoy you or whose life with God you question. What the other person says might complete your thought. In the group time, be respectful of the "pause" questions and allow for the awkward silence to become a holy silence. (If a group member falls asleep during the silence, bless them.) Then share with the group whatever is appropriate for you to share.

Also, be respectful of others as they share, not only because they are made in the image of God but also because the Holy Spirit might see these other people in your group as the best way to get through to you! (See the group guidelines below.) If fifteen sessions are too many for you to go through together as a group, you might want to shorten it to eight by choosing which lessons/parables you especially want to study. You might consider these eight:

- **Lesson 2:** How Jesus Taught (Matthew 13:11–15)
- **Lesson 3:** Why Parables? (Matthew 13:4–19)
- **Lesson 6:** Growing Together in the Kingdom (Matthew 13:24–30; 37–43)
- **Lesson 9:** Lost and Found (Luke 15:11–32)
- **Lesson 11:** The Miracle of Forgiveness (Matthew 18:21–35)
- **Lesson 12:** The Outrageous Compassion of God (Matthew 20:1–16)

- **Lesson 13:** What Is Your Life? (Luke 12:16–21)
- **Lesson 15:** Moved by Compassion (Luke 10:30–37)

As you work through the content, keep the following group guidelines in mind.

- **Be an active listener:** Listen without trying to figure out what someone is going to say (mind reading). Do not talk to others (cross talk) while someone else is sharing. "*To answer before listening—that is folly and shame*" (Proverbs 18:13).

- **Talk about your own issues:** Use "I" statements such as, "I think . . . I feel . . ." Discuss areas where *you* need to change, not where you feel *others* need to change. "*Let your conversation be always full of grace, seasoned with salt, so that you may know how to answer everyone*" (Colossians 4:6).

- **Accept where others are in their journey:** Don't try to "fix" people's problems, and don't give advice to others unless it is requested. Accept others where they are and don't take lightly anyone else's feelings. Don't criticize, condemn, or look down on others. Allow others to cry if they need to do so. "*Accept one another, then, just as Christ accepted you*" (Romans 15:7).

- **Always maintain confidentiality:** Do not allow gossip—what is said in the group . . . stays in the group. Exercise care with what people share and confidentiality in prayer and prayer requests. "*A gossip betrays a confidence, but a trustworthy person keeps a secret*" (Proverbs 11:13).

- **Practice and encourage honesty and openness:** Be as honest and vulnerable as the safety level of the group allows. Avoid presenting an image of looking "okay" and "having it all together." "*My grace is sufficient for you, for my power is made perfect in weakness*" (2 Corinthians 12:9).

- **Take ownership of your own life and growth:** Your journey is your responsibility. You cannot change others, but you can change yourself. "*For each one should carry their own load*" (Galatians 6:5).

Our gracious FATHER, HOLY SPIRIT, Lord JESUS, we are so thankful for the opportunity to explore what you have said about your KINGDOM through these beautiful stories. We pray that you will take them and bless them by your SPIRIT in the POWER of a constant relationship of communication, guidance, love, and service. Plant the SEED of your living WORD deep within us so that our hearing of it may be PROFITABLE to the upbuilding of our soul and to the advancement of your KINGDOM that is available to us all. Help us to receive the grace we need each day to SEE clearly and to HEAR the WORD of the KINGDOM— to the very foundation of our lives.

DALLAS WILLARD

LESSON 1

THE FAITH OF CHRIST

(Mark 4:35–41)

The kingdom of God is now available.

DALLAS WILLARD

As a young minister studying the Bible, Dallas Willard realized something different was going on in the churches around him compared to what went on in the life and ministry of Jesus. The difference was simple: While Jesus hid from people at times, *they* spent thousands of dollars and exhausted themselves trying to get people to come to church. While Jesus said, "Don't let anyone know I did this," *they* begged, cajoled, and pleaded with people to come to church. In spite of Jesus' secrecy, crowds flocked to hear him and were astounded by his life and message.

Dallas found, in his study of the Gospels, Acts, and the epistles, that a substitution had been made. Christians were meant not only to have faith *in* Christ but also to grow to have the faith *of* Christ. To have faith *in* Christ means believing that Jesus is the Son of God; to have the faith *of* Christ means to have the same kind of faith in God that Jesus himself had. To have the faith *of* Christ means having the same confidence that Jesus himself had, which led him to do the things he did—teaching, healing, giving himself to others so completely.

We put our faith *in* Jesus so that we might receive the faith *of* Jesus.

Merely having faith *in* Christ leaves Christ *outside* the believer's personality. This exterior notion of Christ's faith and love are not strong enough to generate the confident statement, "I am crucified with Christ: nevertheless I live; yet not I, but Christ liveth in me: and the life which I now live in the flesh I live by the faith *of* the Son of God, who loved me, and gave himself for me" (Galatians 2:20 KJV, emphasis added).[1]

Believing *in* Christ is a place to start, but as we grow, we are to take the faith Christ had into ourselves, which then radiates throughout every dimension of who we are.[2] But is this really possible? Agnes Sanford, a writer, Bible teacher, and respected facilitator of healing, wrote of an insight she gained about this when she and a friend were staying at the beach in Tiburon, California. A tremendous wind kept shaking the picture window in front of them. She finally shouted, "Okay, that's enough! Quiet down." Agnes wrote, "Suddenly, the wind was still. I cannot explain this! It happened, that's all."[3] This was the faith *of* Christ.

1. What were some of Jesus' miracles that showed his faith (the faith *of* Christ)?

2. Faith is a gift, a seed, to be received, planted, and nurtured. Our faith *in* Christ is a part of, and the *entryway* into, having the faith *of* Christ. In what area of your life would you like to see your faith grow?

Hearing What Jesus Said

To illustrate the difference between having faith *in* Christ and having the faith *of* Christ, consider the following scene on a boat on the Sea of Galilee.

> That day when evening came, he said to his disciples, "Let us go over to the other side." Leaving the crowd behind, they took him along, just as he was, in the boat. There were also other boats with him. A furious squall came up, and the waves broke over the boat, so that it was nearly swamped. Jesus was in the stern, sleeping on a cushion (Mark 4:35–38).

The fact that Jesus could lie down in the middle of a storm and go to sleep is a glimpse of what the faith *of* Christ was like.

> The disciples woke him and said to him, "Teacher, don't you care if we drown?" He got up, rebuked the wind and said to the waves, "Quiet! Be still!" Then the wind died down and it was completely calm. He said to his disciples, "Why are you so afraid? Do you still have no faith?" They were terrified and asked each other, "Who is this? Even the wind and the waves obey him!" (Mark 4:38–41).

The disciples showed their faith *in* Christ by waking him and crying, "Lord, save us! We are perishing!" (Matthew 8:25 NKJV), even though they had not yet seen Jesus interact with nature by calming a storm or feeding a crowd.[4] They relied on him to *do something* in the storm. They had great faith in him, but they did not yet have his great faith in God.[5] They did not have the faith *of* Christ, which would have been strong enough to fend off all fear. To attain the degree of Jesus' faith, they had to enter into the kind of life Jesus had, which was to come.

Jesus' faith was such that he relied on the power of his Father to stop the wind and still the sea just by speaking to it: "Peace! Be still!" This is the faith into which we can grow.

Then, in kindness, Jesus turned to them in their fear, addressing them in that familiar way: "O you of little faith" (Matthew 8:26 ESV). Some people see this as scolding, but elsewhere in the Gospels we see that Jesus had a high opinion of "little faith," saying that faith as small as a mustard seed could move mountains (see Matthew 17:20).

3. Try to imagine Jesus speaking to the wind in a severely rocking boat. In what ways do you admire Jesus—perhaps in his desires, actions, and abilities?

4. In what circumstances would you like the "faith of Christ" (as he had in the boat) to be true of you? For example, what personal storms (such as rejection or failure) would you like to be empowered to calm in yourself or others?

Thinking About What Jesus Said

The Message of Christ: The Kingdom of God

The idea that you can have the faith *of* Christ might seem overwhelming. Can you *really* have a life with God to the extent you trust him—and act in the same kind of faith in him—as Jesus did? You are more likely to grow to this point as you understand that you can live in the everlasting kingdom of God here and now. It's not off in the future. It is present *right now*.

Dallas Willard noticed this other "substitution" as he studied the Bible to see why today's churches are not as effective as the church was in Acts. He saw that people were being taught a message *about* Christ (who he was and what he did) instead of the message *of* Christ (the one that Jesus himself preached).

What did Jesus preach, exactly? Dallas saw clearly in his study of Jesus' sermons that his message was about the kingdom of God and how it was available to everyone with his arrival. It had always existed in the past (see Psalm 145:13), but when Jesus came, he brought it more fully. It will come in even greater power and glory when he returns.

Here is what Jesus said: "From that time Jesus began to preach, and to say, Repent: for the kingdom of heaven is at hand'" (Matthew 4:17 KJV; see also Matthew 3:2; 10:7; Mark 1:15). Many people think this means that we should *feel sorry for our sins because the kingdom of God is coming some day*. But when Jesus said the kingdom was "at hand," he meant it the same way that someone today might extend his or her hand toward the dining room and say to a guest, "Here's the dining room." Jesus was telling his listeners that the kingdom of God was present among them in his own self (see Matthew 4:17).

When Jesus said to people that they needed to repent, he was telling them to reconsider how they had been approaching their lives now that they could live in his presence and take his life into their own. They could embrace the abundant kingdom with a clear-eyed vision of a totally good and competent God who was right there looking after them.

5. Notice the kingdom of God is described as *abundant*, *available*, and *accessible* and that we can live with a *clear-eyed vision of a good and competent God who is looking after us*. Which of these descriptions is most interesting to you? Why?

6. Consider the following views of repentance: "feeling sorry for sin" and "reconsidering how they had been approaching their life now that they could live in the presence of Jesus." How is a person affected differently by each view?

The Presence of Christ: The Kingdom of God

When the Pharisees once asked Jesus when the kingdom of God would come, Christ replied, "The coming of the kingdom of God is not something that can be observed, nor will people say, 'Here it is,' or 'There it is,' because the kingdom of God is in your midst" (Luke 17:20–21). Jesus was teaching them that the kingdom of God was not an institution or building they could see but was Jesus himself "in their midst." As people looked at him and listened to him, they saw the kingdom and its availability *in him*.

What is the kingdom of God? It's the range of God's effective will. It exists wherever what God *wants* done is *actually* done. It is simply God acting in this world: "Thy kingdom come, Thy will be done" (Matthew 6:10 KJV). Jesus put a face on the kingdom of God.

What does it mean that the kingdom of God is available to us here and now? The author of Hebrews provided the following encouragement to people who had endured trial and hardship: "Therefore, since we are receiving a kingdom that cannot be shaken, let us be thankful, and so worship God acceptably with reverence and awe" (Hebrews 12:28). In our everyday existence, we live in the invisible but invincible and unshakable kingdom of God. Even in our worst moments, we have the strong presence of Christ holding us up. In the kingdom, God can redeem our worst moments so that what seems like the last thing we would want to happen moves to first place as a pivotal moment for which we can be thankful. (Give it time, though!)

As we live in the kingdom, our actions and the words we use to bless others or overcome evil are filled with God's power. In those moments, we are partnering with God to impart renewed life to others. This happens as we teach the kingdom of God through Jesus' life and wisdom, especially his parables specifically about the kingdom of God.

All that is required to usher us into the kingdom of God is the sincere willingness of our hearts to follow Christ by the grace and power of God. As we learn how to live fully in the kingdom of God in the here and now, we become his disciples and friends (see John 15:15), working and living out of kingdom resources.

7. When have you experienced the kingdom of God—that is, you saw something done that you knew was the kind of thing God wants people to do here on earth?

8. What might it look like for you to be "working and living out of kingdom resources"? Think big!

Understanding Kingdom Language

A human kingdom is a society led by a king or queen who serves the good of the people by providing them with care, protection, and service. The kingdom of God is exactly like that. The Trinity—Father, Son, and Holy Spirit—loves us and works for our good. While citizens of a human kingdom offer loyalty, service, and respect to their monarch, we offer our love, worship, and obedience to God. One of the many differences is that human government generally rules by using force, deception, brutality, and the threat of punishment (sometimes including the death penalty). Human government lacks the power of life, which is what the kingdom of God specializes in—leading us to "life that is truly life" (1 Timothy 6:19).

The kingdom of God is not like any human government. It is from everlasting to everlasting; it cannot be shaken and is totally good (see Psalm 145:13; Daniel 7:14; Hebrews 12:28). It has never been in trouble and never will be.[6] Jesus' teaching reveals to us that the kingdom of God is not a thing of time and place but is a thing of the heart. It is a life that is lived in vital connection with God himself.

We are invited to bring our life into the eternal life of God in his everlasting kingdom, being mindful that eternity is already in progress and is not something that will start later. In fact, the only biblical definition of eternal life is this: "That they may know You, the only true God, and Jesus Christ whom You have sent" (John 17:3 NKJV). The phrase "know you" is an *interactive* and *experiential* relationship, and everything that we bring into that relationship becomes eternal. In that way, we live an eternal kind of life here and now.

When we live in the kingdom of God by the Spirit of God, our lives overflow with goodness and mercy. We are not the ones who make this happen. It is a gift from God; we merely receive it. It moves far beyond what we eat and drink and plunges us into righteousness, peace, and joy in the Holy Spirit, which is not humanly possible (see Romans 14:17). The best advice about how to go to heaven is *to go now* by living your life with God.

9. How do you respond to the idea that God wants you to have a life of interacting with him—one that is relational and experiential—rather than just having head knowledge about him? What would it look like for you to have that kind of life with God?

10. In what shaky life circumstances (unstable relationships, beginning a new adventure, uncertain future) do you need to immerse yourself in the truth that you "are receiving a kingdom that cannot be shaken" (Hebrews 12:28)? Be specific.

Responding to What Jesus Said

An Open Invitation to Everyone

You may be surprised to learn that you can grow into having the faith *of* Christ and are living in the strong and unshakable kingdom of God right now. It is easy to think of yourself (or someone else) as not being *qualified* to have and do these things. Jesus knew this and went out of his way to stress the openness of the kingdom and the ease with which anyone could enter.

We see this "anyone factor" in the story of a leper who came to Jesus and asked to be healed. Lepers were not supposed to be *coming toward* people. They were required to *move away* from people. Jesus violated the protocols for leprosy in even talking with a leper. Yet this diseased man, who was supposed to stay away from people, had heard Jesus teach. So he came to Jesus and asked, "Lord, if you are willing, you can make me clean." The leper was prepared to be rejected, because he had undoubtedly experienced a lot of rejection. So, he said, "*If* you are willing . . ." Jesus answered, "I *am* willing" (Matthew 8:2–3, emphasis added). Jesus' disregard of common custom was unheard of in the eyes of people in that day.

This kind of radical acceptance and interaction with others reinforced the message that Jesus preached about the present availability of the kingdom of God to all. Nothing that you ever have done nor any opinions that others have formed about you disqualifies you from growing into the faith *of* Christ, from living in the kingdom of God here and now, or from having an interactive and experiential relationship with God. You were built for these things, and God is eager for you to join in this kind of life.

11. How would you describe Jesus' personality and behavior in his encounter with the leper? Is there anything there you admire? Explain your response.

12. Write down three actions taken or words spoken that would seem to disqualify a person from entrance into God's kingdom. Pause after each and say, "Everyone is welcome in the kingdom of God."

Key Terms

Kingdom of God: The range of God's effective will; anyplace where what God wants done actually gets done.

Eternal life / eternal living: Knowing the only true God and his Son as an interactive, experiential relationship resulting in a life caught up in the life of God (see John 17:3).

Faith of Christ: The kind of faith that Christ possessed that enabled him to teach as he taught and do as he did (see Galatians 2:20).

For Further Reading

Dallas Willard, "Flesh and Spirit," chapter 3 in *Renewing the Christian Mind: Essays, Interviews, and Talks* (San Francisco: HarperOne, 2016), on the faith of Christ.

Dallas Willard, *The Divine Conspiracy: Rediscovering Our Hidden Life in God* (New York: HarperCollins, 1998), chapter 4, on what is the gospel.

John Bright, *The Kingdom of God* (Nashville, TN: Abingdon Press, 1980).

George Eldon Ladd, "What Is the Kingdom of God?", chapter 1 in *The Gospel of the Kingdom: Scriptural Studies in the Kingdom of God* (Grand Rapids, MI: Wm. B. Eerdmans, 1959).

Notes

1. Some translations say "faith in Christ." This is a controversial issue among translators. Some recent versions say "the faithfulness of Christ." Other translations that state "faith of Christ/Son of God" include the Twenty-First Century King James Version, Jubilee Bible 2000, New Revised Standard Version: Updated Edition, and Young's Literal Translation.
2. Adapted from Dallas Willard, "Spiritual Formation and the Warfare Between the Flesh and the Human Spirit," *Journal of Spiritual Formation and Soul Care*, vol. 1, no. 1 (Spring 2008), 84. This article was reprinted in *Renewing the Christian Mind* (San Francisco: HarperOne Publishers, 2016), 62.
3. Agnes Sanford, *Sealed Orders* (Monroe, LA: Logos International, 1972), 308–309.
4. This event occurred well into Jesus' second year of ministry before he walked on water or fed the group of five thousand.
5. Dallas Willard, *Hearing God: Developing a Conversational Life with God* (Lisle, IL: InterVarsity Press, 2012), 203.
6. Willard, *The Divine Conspiracy: Rediscovering Our Hidden Life in God* (New York: HarperCollins, 1998), 25.

LESSON 2

HOW JESUS TAUGHT

(Matthew 13:11–15)

The genius of Jesus as a teacher is clearly seen in
his respectful and merciful approach.

DALLAS WILLARD

The realizations that we grow into having the faith *of* Christ and that we live in a strong and unshakable kingdom of God helped Dallas Willard understand that if we want to have the results that Jesus had, we need to teach what Christ taught and teach it in the manner in which he taught it. To help us to do this, we will examine not only the content of the parables about the kingdom of God but also the manner in which Jesus approached his teaching.

Many people misunderstand *what* Jesus taught because they don't understand *how* he taught it. Jesus didn't teach the way the leaders in his day taught. He was a capable but creative and playful teacher. Grasping his approach helps us interpret his words correctly (know the truth) and teach in the manner in which he taught (teach the truth).

First, *Jesus taught a way of life, not regulations*. He didn't offer lists of do's and don'ts for us to keep. Such lists lead to legalism, which is far from the relational approach of learning to live in the kingdom day by day, moment by moment, comfortably in the care of God. His teachings went far deeper than laws; they were aimed at the heart. He didn't speak only of correct behaviors but moved to the center of the person's being and practically to their whole-life condition. In this way, he showed us what it's like to live under the direction of God.

Second, *Jesus used stories, not arguments*. When Jesus was attacked by people for what was considered culturally unacceptable behavior, such as having conversations with lepers or dining with tax collectors and sinners, he didn't defend himself directly. Instead, he slipped around people's defenses by telling simple stories that showed his listeners the attractive openness of the kingdom. These stories about everyday occurrences, such as family disputes or farming situations, provided clarity about what the kingdom of God was like. A shepherd sought a lost sheep, a woman sought a lost coin, and a father sought a lost son (see Luke 15:3–32). By entering into these situations through stories, people gained a greater sense of the kingdom of God and how it worked.

Jesus intentionally used the following methods to help his listeners *truly hear*, *remember*, *ponder deeply*, and *embrace* what he said:

- **Cultural relevance:** Jesus sought to challenge and radically change the prevailing presumptions of his day (that is, the things people believed and lived without even thinking about it).

- **Easily remembered:** In Jesus' stories, people behaved in unusual ways, which made the stories difficult to forget. He also left many parables open-ended, asking listeners to think about what would happen next.

- **In the context of ordinary life:** Jesus used everyday objects and activities his listeners were familiar with to ease them in. Often he didn't sound "religious."

- **More meaningful as time passed:** The impact of parables was like yeast that kept expanding over time. People needed time to fully work out what Jesus said and grow in the truth the parables were communicating.

1. What are some reasons that Jesus taught through illustrations and stories?

2. Which of the four methods that Jesus used in his teaching is most interesting to you? Why that particular method?

Hearing What Jesus Said

After Jesus told some of his first parables to the crowd, the baffled disciples asked him, "Why do you speak to the people in parables?" (Matthew 13:10). Jesus answered:

> "To you it has been given to know the secrets of the kingdom of heaven, but to them *it has not been given*. For to those who have, more will be given, and they will have an abundance, but from those who have nothing, even what they have will be taken away. The reason I speak to them in parables is that 'seeing they do not perceive, and hearing they do not listen, nor do they understand.' With them indeed is fulfilled the prophecy of Isaiah that says:
>
> 'You will indeed listen but never understand,
> and you will indeed look but never perceive.
> For this people's heart has grown dull,
> and their ears are hard of hearing,
> and they have shut their eyes,
> so that they might not look with their eyes,
> and hear with their ears
> and understand with their heart and turn—
> and I would heal them'" (Matthew 13:11–15 NRSVUE, emphasis added).

Jesus had a strategy. He knew that stories help us receive the message so as to enlarge our capacity to hear truth. So why did he say that knowing the secrets of the kingdom had not been given to them? Notice that he did *not* say, "I'm not going to *give* you understanding," but, "it has not *been given*." Jesus gave his listeners only as much understanding of what he said as they had the capacity to receive. Picture this: If a person takes a bucket to get water from a faucet, he or she can get only the amount of water that fills the bucket. The folks to whom Jesus spoke didn't have very big buckets, so to speak, so he couldn't give them very much.

The next phrase, "For to those who have, more will be given . . . from those who have nothing, even what they have will be taken away" is based on the logical reasoning that students who *want* to learn will continue acquiring more insight, while those who don't want to learn lose even the insight they have. Now picture this: A person doesn't have a bucket ("but from those who have nothing," not attuned to receiving), but he or she might try to hold the water with cupped hands. Of course, it will be lost ("even what they have will be taken away").

Jesus was unwilling to give his listeners more than they wanted to know or could absorb because it wouldn't help them. Through parables, he gave people only as much truth as they could stand or absorb. The more readiness to receive from God a person has, the more they will receive; however, if a person is not receptive, that readiness usually disappears. God reached out in love and humility, without coercion.

3. How do Jesus' words in Matthew 13:11–15 explain why some people seem to get more out of what he said (and the Bible in general) than others?

4. What do you think affects people's capacity to receive truth?

Thinking About What Jesus Said

Jesus, the Respectful Genius

Jesus never dropped spiritual bombs on people but instead told them stories, such as, "Let's say there were two sons. The younger one wanted his inheritance *now*. His father simply gave it to him" (Luke 15:11–12, paraphrase). They could relate to a story about a family.

Jesus' parables were an act of mercy to those whose hearts were hard (distracted, resistant, cynical). Jesus told the above story about the prodigal son after the Pharisees had criticized him for fraternizing with tax collectors, who were not known for their great faith. Jesus knew that if he directly challenged the hard hearts of the Pharisees, their hearts would become even harder. So instead, he told a story that invited reflection, not objections.

In so doing, Jesus didn't assault people's minds by throwing religion at them. He didn't condemn them, because he knew people were already condemning themselves (see John 3:17). He respectfully let people come to their own conclusions because he knew God had placed in the hands of every person the key to his or her own heart. It unlocks only from the inside. God will not force a heart open, but he will offer something that helps people unlock it.

Jesus was aware that the people's hardness of hearts was connected to their will. They didn't *want* to hear or understand. But he didn't give up on them; he chose to give them what they *could* receive. When he said, "I speak to them in parables, because seeing they do not see, and hearing they do not hear, nor do they understand" (Matthew 13:13 ESV), he was probably thinking, *At this moment they aren't ready to hear or see. But if I tell them a story about a woman who searched her entire house for one lost precious object, they will remember it for a while, and the deeper meaning will reveal itself in time.*

Jesus' teaching style provided people with the opportunity to take responsibility for opening the door to their own hearts, seeking the truth, and hunting for even more truth. By the time his listeners were able to discern the truth for themselves (rather than being lectured at), they may have even been able to stand it! Jesus' respectful and merciful approach to teaching shows his genius as a teacher. He didn't just deliver information; he presented people with a different kind of life than that to which they were accustomed. This gave them a vision of how life in the kingdom of God fit into their everyday, ordinary life.

5. What do you admire the most about Jesus as a teacher? Why that trait?

6. How are listeners affected when a person shares truth with respect and mercy, just as Jesus did? How have you witnessed this in your own life?

The Great Inversion

Jesus' teachings often directly opposed people's common beliefs and opinions. They were so revolutionary that people thought he was trying to disregard God's laws and prophecies, so he had to clarify and say, "Do not think that I have come to abolish the Law or the Prophets" (Matthew 5:17). Even though his parables approached people gently, they often contained details that seemed scandalous. They often described the kingdom of God as nothing like what the people expected. In fact, they seemed the opposite!

Jesus' picture of truth has been called the "Great Inversion" because it seemed to turn people's ordinary ideas upside down. In the kingdom, disgraceful, rebellious sons were welcomed home, but the highly regarded rich men had trouble getting into heaven (see Luke 15:20–24; Matthew 19:23). Workers who toiled only one hour got paid the same as those who worked all day (see Matthew 20:1–16). This Great Inversion is well expressed by these words: "Many who are first will be last, and many who are last will be first" (Matthew 19:30).

Jesus lived that Great Inversion as well. He constantly associated with immoral people: "Now all the tax collectors and sinners were coming near to listen to him" (Luke 15:1 NRSVUE). He not only welcomed them but, even worse, also ate with them! To many people in Jesus' day, especially the Pharisees and the scribes, one of the most repulsive things about him was his habit of eating with objectionable people whether they washed their hands or not. In that culture, those with whom you chose to eat said everything about your character, so to eat with notorious people made Jesus disreputable. To make matters worse, Jesus said on one occasion that these dishonorable people would get into the kingdom of God before those who thought themselves to be righteous (see Matthew 21:31).

Jesus' welcoming nature showcased the remarkable generosity of God. He was comfortable with the "wrong people" because he was situated solidly in the kingdom of God. He could be with *anyone*; he could be *anywhere*. This isn't necessarily true of us, but as we grow as his disciples and enter deeper into his kind of life, we can increasingly be like him—perfectly safe and perfectly strong in the kingdom of God.

7. How would you describe the Great Inversion in your own words—maybe in humorous terms or the way you would explain it to a five-year-old?

8. Jesus, by being situated in the kingdom of God, was able to be anywhere with any kind of person. How have you found the same to be true in your life?

Teaching to Transform

The goal of great teaching is not to impart loads of information or to inspire people with eloquence but to present listeners with words and experiences that will impact the active flow of their lives. One way Jesus accomplished this was by teaching in the context of ordinary life. Instead of referring to religious ideas and sacred objects, he illustrated truth from common occupations and daily activities. He talked about things such as money, fruit, vines, feasts, seeds, coins, trees, and sheep. Everybody could understand and identify with what he was saying ("Yes, I've lost a sheep!"). This made the kingdom of God more accessible to them.

Great teachers say things in ways that ensure their teaching is easily remembered. Jesus' audience didn't have the benefit of computers, records, handouts, or even pens like we have—they had to be able to "get it" just from listening. So Jesus found ways to shake people up a bit by poking holes in what they already believed. He got right to the heart of the assumptions and practices common to the culture of the day and tweaked them. The people didn't have to try to remember what he said, because it puzzled them enough to stay with it.

In general, the practical way that Jesus taught was to take whatever idea was floating by and puncture a hole in it. Imagine how the people felt when they heard, "It is easier for a camel to go through the eye of a needle than for someone who is rich to enter the kingdom of God" (Matthew 19:24). The culture of the day taught that rich people were God's favorites. But when Jesus was invited to dinner with a house full of wealthy neighbors and relatives, he said to the host, "When you have a dinner, don't invite your relatives and your wealthy neighbors" (see Luke 14:12). The host didn't think, *Let me write that down so I can remember it.* Everyone who was listening would have been struck by this contradiction to what they believed. This is why people remembered it—and because they remembered it, it changed their lives.

Some people, however, rejected Jesus' message, choosing to close their ears and shut their eyes. We may wonder, *Why didn't God just make them open their ears?* The reason is because Jesus did not force people to hear. "Love is not rude or pushy" (1 Corinthians 13:5, paraphrase). Parables allowed Jesus' listeners to choose to hear or not hear, to see or not see.

9. How did Jesus go beyond teaching that was just informational in nature?

10. Imagine that you were one of the people in the crowd listening to Jesus' teaching. How do you think that you would have responded? Would you have been offended? Intrigued? Dismissive? Having to sit down and think about it? Explain your response.

Responding to What Jesus Said

Reflective Space

The Holy Spirit is our teacher as we read Scripture. The Bible was not given to us as a book of instructions independent of his leading. When we try to understand it on our own, "the letter kills." Jesus knew this and taught in a way that people would be led by the Spirit into a realm of reality—the kingdom of God—because "the Spirit gives life" (2 Corinthians 3:6).

Jesus' stories allowed people time and space to think so that the Holy Spirit might have time to work, circumventing their pride or fear. A story invites reflection, not argument. This is why we need to meditate on the parables, asking the Spirit to help us and allowing our understanding to grow. So, before you answer the questions in this workbook related to each parable, take some time to first pause and reflect. Notice any words or phrases in the parable that stand out to you, and then ask God why those particular words resonated with you. With this interaction, your personal relationship with God will deepen as it creates conversation with God. This will help you to learn to love the guidance of the Holy Spirit in understanding truth.

The Parable of the Sower that we will cover in the next lesson—with its soils representing a life of easy distractions, a lack of focus, and competing demands—may cause you to see yourself as one of those soils (see Matthew 13:4–9, 18–19). But that may also take time. Jesus' parables will work like yeast in you, tucked away in your mind and expanding, and will become more meaningful as your understanding expands with the passing of time. Jesus' parables plant seeds in the mind and soul of every listener, slowly sprouting and taking form, bringing them into another kingdom in which a different kind of life prevails.

11. How would you assess yourself on the following continuum? (If you are not sure, take a moment to ask someone in your household to tell you!)

I can stay focused and get things done . . . now!	I often get distracted by everything there is to do.

12. How do you think this might impact your ability to sync with the Holy Spirit? How might you invite the Spirit to help you and give you focus as you explore Jesus' parables?

Key Terms

Culture: Ideas people believe without always thinking about them and actions they take that require no explanation or justification.[1]

Great Inversion: In the kingdom of God, there is a reversal of order from the human kingdom, not the least of which is "the transformation of status for the lowly, the humanly hopeless, as they experience the hand of God reaching into their situation."[2] "There are none in the humanly 'down' position so low that they cannot be lifted up by entering God's order, and none in the humanly 'up' position so high that they can disregard God's point of view on their lives."[3]

Parable: The word *parable* comes from the Greek words *para*, meaning "beside" (as in parallel lines) and *bole*, which means "to throw or to place." Teaching by parables means placing two things next to each other to learn more about them through contrast and comparison.

For Further Reading

Dallas Willard, "Jesus, the Logician," chapter 15 in *The Great Omission: Reclaiming Jesus' Essential Teachings on Discipleship* (San Francisco: HarperOne, 2006).

George Eldon Ladd, "The Mystery of the Kingdom," chapter 4 in *The Gospel of the Kingdom: Scriptural Studies in the Kingdom of God* (Grand Rapids, MI: Wm. B. Eerdmans, 1959).

Kenneth Bailey, "Introduction to the Parables," chapter 21 in *Jesus Through Middle Eastern Eyes: Cultural Studies in the Gospels* (Lisle, IL: InterVarsity Press, 2008).

Klyne Snodgrass, *Stories with Intent: A Comprehensive Guide to the Parables of Jesus* (Grand Rapids, MI: Wm. B. Eerdmans, 2018), a textbook on the parables.

Notes

1. Willard, *The Divine Conspiracy*, 260.
2. Willard, *The Divine Conspiracy*, Kindle edition, 137.
3. Willard, *The Divine Conspiracy*, 89.

LESSON 3

WHY PARABLES?

Parable of the Sower (Matthew 13:4–19)

The mind, and what we turn our minds to, is the key to our lives.

DALLAS WILLARD

Jesus could have taught about the four different kinds of listening in the Parable of the Sower in Matthew 13:4–19 very differently. He could have drawn a chart in the air, describing the four levels of receptivity, or he could have labeled them with first-century equivalents to letter grades (A, B, C, D). But instead, he chose something people saw every day: different kinds of dirt! The four kinds of soil described in the Parable of the Sower illustrate a person's willingness to hear the message, reflect on it, embrace it, and live in it.

Receptivity is important because the gentle Word of God will not knock us over. We will not recognize it if we don't listen with care, but we can learn to recognize it if we desire it and make space for it. Some people have misunderstood the seeds' responses to the soil as describing what happens only when people first encounter God: acceptance or rejection. But it's more than that. As disciples, we find it applies to us all the time. What kind of soil are we *today*? Does the Word of God bounce off our hardened wayside soil, get choked by thorns, or get crowded out by stones? Or is it willingly received in the fertile, airy good soil?

When these circumstances are limited to first-time encounters with God's truth, this parable is often read fatalistically. It's expected that three-fourths of people who hear will turn away, since the seed does not flourish in three out of the four soils. But that was not Jesus' intent. He is seeking all of us. God's initiative is assertive! Jesus next words were, "No one after lighting a lamp covers it over with a container" (Luke 8:16, paraphrase). The Sower of the Word (God) never intends that the lamp of the Word be covered up. It is to be lifted up (set on a lampstand) to give light to everyone in the house. This happens in us as we receive the Word of the kingdom into our lives and live *in* it, shedding light wherever we are.

Humility is required in this because we often think we already know, when in fact we don't truly know. When Jesus came, he said, "Forget what you think you know about God, because no one knows the Father except the Son and the one to whom the Son wills to reveal him" (Matthew 11:27, paraphrase). People make the mistake of thinking they are going to understand God or his Word by being scholarly, intelligent, and quick, or even by studying hard. But the truth is that the interaction of God with us through his Word is a personal matter. It depends on the condition of our hearts, our minds, and our lives.

All the above—receptivity, humility, and willingness to interact with God—point to the "set" of our mind. We aren't prisoners of our mind; we can change our way of thinking. Indeed, as Dallas Willard wrote, "the first freedom we have is where we put our mind."[1] Even a prisoner of war has that one freedom. Every day, we make this choice many times.

1. Why is it important to interact with God about how he is revealing himself to you?

2. How do you respond to the statement that "the first freedom we have is where we put our mind"? Do you believe that you can change your way of thinking? Why or why not?

Hearing What Jesus Said

As Jesus' ministry progressed, he noticed the different reactions that people had to what he was saying. Not everyone could receive his words, and those who did receive them responded in different ways. The people whose hearts were concerned with always getting what they wanted in life were hardened by the message that he came to bring. He sensed their resistance. The Parable of the Sower portrays the different reactions of people to his teaching.

As you read through this parable, notice that there is not one religious word in the story. Jesus didn't read Scripture or pray. He just told the people a story in the context of the ordinary life of a farmer who was planting seed. (Refer to the key terms in this lesson for an explanation of what Jesus meant by "the word of God" or "the word of the kingdom.")

> On the same day Jesus went out of the house and sat by the sea. And great multitudes were gathered together to Him, so that He got into a boat and sat; and the whole multitude stood on the shore.
>
> Then He spoke many things to them in parables, saying: "Behold, a sower went out to sow. And as he sowed, some seed fell by the wayside; and the birds came and devoured them. Some fell on stony places, where they did not have much earth; and they immediately sprang up because they had no depth of earth. But when the sun was up they were scorched,

> and because they had no root they withered away. And some fell among thorns, and the thorns sprang up and choked them. But others fell on good ground and yielded a crop: some a hundredfold, some sixty, some thirty. He who has ears to hear, let him hear!" (Matthew 13:1–9 NKJV).
>
> "Therefore hear the parable of the sower: When anyone hears the *word of the kingdom*, and does not understand it, then the wicked one comes and snatches away what was sown in his heart. This is he who received seed by the wayside. But he who received the seed on stony places, this is he who *hears the word* and immediately receives it with joy" (Matthew 13:18–20 NKJV, emphasis added).

The Parable of the Sower is one of the most important parables that Jesus gave about the kingdom of God because it answers the question, "Why doesn't the Word (*logos*) have the effect on people that we hope it would?"[2] It moves us to ask again why God doesn't just change people. But the point is not about what God *can* do but about what God *will* do. It is about the precise manner of how God chooses to interact with people to accomplish his purposes in this world. It is true that the God of all the earth can do anything he wants, but there are a lot of things that God doesn't want to do, including creating people who are religious robots. He desires for us to learn and grow freely.

3. What does it say about Jesus that he didn't use religious language or ideas in this parable (which was likely his first)? Or that he explained it only to his disciples who asked?

4. Be honest . . . do you wish that God would just change people? Or that God were more pushy when it comes to dealing with people? Explain your response.

Thinking About What Jesus Said

Wayside Soil

Looking at how seeds grow or don't grow in the Parable of the Sower illustrates why people react the way they do to the Word of the kingdom. Those living like the soils on the wayside, stony ground, and thorny ground are not able to let the Word work at a deep level in their soul. They have the privilege and responsibility of receiving it, but they do so in a limited way.

The birds scouring the wayside ground show the work of the wicked one, who doesn't want people to truly hear the message. C. S. Lewis described in *The Screwtape Letters* how people are enslaved "to the pressure of the ordinary." The main character in the story was thinking deeply about God and was about to conclude that God was real, but then it struck him that it was lunchtime. He didn't pursue the thought any further.[3] The mind is easily distracted.

The wicked one may also distort the Word. For example, if we think the invitation of God means that he will provide easy solutions to our problems, then we might try to use the message for our purposes—to get what we want. This involves no inward turning toward God, no inner turning from self toward others. There is no humility and surrender to the truth. The result is that we remain shallow and are simply using God. When a little trouble comes, we complain, "This is not what I had in mind. No, thank you. I'll just leave."

The enemy also works through loneliness. Mother Teresa of Calcutta wrote, "In the West there is so much loneliness. . . . The greatest disease in the West today is . . . being unwanted, unloved, and uncared for."[4] The wicked one is busily working to keep people apart. In workplaces, families, schools, and even churches, people believe that if they don't get along with certain people, they should just simply have nothing to do with them.

Thoughts like these come to us again and again. We are so busy doing things our way that we can't hear any messages of love, unity, forgiveness, and acceptance. They just get whisked out of our minds.

5. Consider the main character in C. S. Lewis's story who was thinking deeply about God but then got distracted. What would wisdom look like in that situation he described?

6. What other kinds of thoughts does the wicked one use to distract us in addition to those already mentioned (ordinary daily events, distorting God's Word, trying to get what we want, loneliness)? Which of these does he particularly use against you?

Stony Soil, Thorny Soil, Good Soil

Upon hearing the Word, those whose hearts represent the stony soil say, "I love it! This is wonderful!" But it does not penetrate the depths of their personality. The seeds don't take root because stones block the way. Sometimes those stones are *feelings*. Some people hear God's good news and feel joy, tenderness, or gratitude, but then their feelings change. Feelings sometimes rule character. Character involves long-running patterns of behavior from which our actions automatically arise.[5] It's what runs our life. It shows itself in our thinking, choices, habits, and actions that become obvious in our relationships.

In the thorny ground, the *logos* actually takes root! But then such things as riches and cares of this life crowd out the *logos* with the worries of life, the deceitfulness of wealth, the desire of other things, and the pleasures of this life (see Matthew 13:22; Mark 4:19; Luke 8:14). The thorns represent things that keep us too preoccupied to give thought to the Word. We look at our phones as soon as we wake up. Following the news cycle becomes a hard and fast "should." We get so busy accomplishing things that we cannot hear the Word of God's kingdom.

Wealth itself isn't exactly the problem, but rather the lure or deceitfulness of wealth. Our tendency with riches is to think about them and trust in them. One test for considering whether we are in bondage to material goods, including food and clothing, is to consider how much of our time and our best thinking we give to those things. If they are uppermost in our mind, then those thoughts run our life. Their complexity can wear us out.

Seeds sown in the *good soil* receive the Word with "an honest and good heart" (Luke 8:15 NRSVUE). This means not only truly hearing the Word but also seeing its goodness, holding on to it, and acting in connection with it. We join our will with the Word that we've received. This results in an abundant harvest: thirty, sixty, a hundred times more (see Matthew 13:8).

It is the difference in our heart that makes the difference in how the Word affects our lives. This is one of the ways that the *will* affects how we hear. We bring the reality of God into our lives by making contact with him through our *minds*, and our actions are based on the understanding and fullness of that contact.

7. What do you think is involved in having an "honest and good heart" that is receptive to the Word of the kingdom?

8. Given that the Parable of the Sower applies to each of us all the time, how would you describe your soil lately? (Check all that apply.)

- ❑ You are easily distracted by other things—things that are possibly set before you by the wicked one (wayside soil).
- ❑ You like what you read in the Bible, hear in a sermon, or learn about God, but don't dwell on it (stony soil).
- ❑ You like what you read in the Bible, hear in a sermon, or learn about God, but there are so many other concerns . . . (thorny soil).
- ❑ You take what you read in the Bible, hear in a sermon, or learn about God and reflect on how God is inviting you to act on it (good soil).

Why did you choose that particular description (or descriptions)?

Interaction of the Mind and Will

The Word of God that we study and meditate on is a creative, sustaining, and active power. When it comes into our minds, we decide how important it is to hold on to it. This is why the first important question is, "What are you choosing to do with the Word that has come into your mind?" If your will is set against the Word of God, you will get nowhere in understanding it. This parable is about how the will responds to the Word of God—if it "holds on to it."

In biblical language the *will*, the *spirit*, and the *heart* are the same fundamental component of the person. But these three words refer to different aspects of the same thing (see the key terms in this lesson for an explanation). In particular, the *heart* in biblical terms does not refer to feelings as it does in contemporary culture.

The will/heart/spirit can be set on believing that we don't need help, that we don't need other people, and that we are doing fine. But the humble person reaches out for connection. As we use our power of choice to turn our minds to

God, we learn to listen to God throughout the day—all day long—in the midst of everything we do.

The set of our will is key for how the Word of God affects our mind because the will and mind are deeply integrated. What the mind dwells on determines what the will chooses to act on. On the other hand, the orientation of the will may determine what stays in the mind. So it is important to ask ourselves, *What is my mind dwelling on—and why is it dwelling there?*

The mind, and what we turn our mind to, is the key to our lives. Our mind can get clogged with thoughts, ideas, and opinions that are misleading, false, or wrong. In our fallen condition, our mind often does not think the thoughts we need to think, which disables our will from turning to God. An essential investment of our life with God is thus to take care of our minds by cultivating God-centered thoughts. The unkempt mind becomes obsessive, and then the will works from those frenzied thoughts. We can't let just anything run through our minds. When tempted, we have to say to ourselves, *There are some thoughts that I will not think!*

9. How do you "hold on to" the Word that comes into your mind (through reading, listening, or seemingly by "chance" as the Holy Spirit moves in your life)?

10. Do you agree with the statement that "the mind, and what we turn our mind to, is the key to our lives"? Why or why not?

Responding to What Jesus Said

A Hearing Kind of Life

The Word of God comes and fills our lives if we want it to do so, but we have to want it and seek it. If we don't want it, God will allow us to live the "with ourselves" life (the source of all our troubles) instead of the "with God" life (which is a life of growth and abundance).

The Word of God comes to us in a "hearing" kind of life—a life that is lived in the Spirit with a mind attuned to the Trinity. Jesus (the living Word) is the Sower, but he works with people, speaking through them to sow the Word of the kingdom into our lives. Of course, God also speaks to us through the written Word (the Bible). In fact, God's speaking to us most commonly occurs in conjunction with study of and reflection on the Bible. We study and meditate on Scripture in fellowship with the living Word, the Lord himself. As we read and study it intelligently, humbly, and openly, we increasingly come to share God's mind.[6] But if we don't listen with care, even what we've heard may be lost.

When we seek the Word of God, we become the kind of people who are able to hear God's voice. His Word will not be a to-do list: "Do this!" or "Do that!" Most of what God says to us comes in the form of insights that shine a light on what is happening around us. Being attuned to hearing God's Word and receiving it into the fertile soil of our life comes from a life marked by friendship with and confidence in God.

If this sounds out of reach to you, but you desire it, be encouraged that it matters in what direction you are moving—toward God or away from him. So, the question is . . . which way are you facing at this moment?

11. What do you think makes people *want* to hear God and the Word of God?

12. Think of a verse, passage, or Jesus-like idea that has come to you recently. Take a few minutes to sit outside, by a window, or in a comfortable place and consider (1) why this is important to you, and (2) what God may be inviting you to do as a result of it. Record your reflections in the space below.

Key Terms

Word of God: The "Word of God" (or "word of the kingdom") can refer to one or all of these things: (1) Jesus as the living Word of God, (2) the Bible as the written word of God, (3) the preaching and passing on of the Word of God (see Acts 12:24), and/or (4) the Word of God that is "settled in heaven," as the psalmist says (see Psalm 119:89), expressing itself in the order of nature (see Psalm 19:1–4). All of these represent God's Word, as well as his speaking to us when we individually hear from him.[7]

***Logos*:** The word *logos* is derived from the Greek word *lego*, which refers to the structuring and forming of things. *Logos* conveys that this formation is being done now—present tense. When Jesus said "the Word," he used the word *logos* because he was talking about a personal power that was going forth. Jesus was referring to himself as "the logos." "In the beginning was the Word" (John 1:1), the *Logos*, who was Jesus.[8]

Will/heart/spirit: If we set aside contemporary prejudices and carefully examine the two great sources of knowledge, Judeo-Christian (biblical) and Greek (classical), it becomes clear that *heart*, *spirit*, and *will* (or their equivalents) refer to one and the same fundamental component of the person. But they do so under different aspects. *Will* refers to that component's power to initiate, create, or bring about what did not exist before. *Spirit* refers to its fundamental nature as distinct and independent from physical reality. *Heart* refers to its position in the human being, as the core to which every other component of the self owes its proper functioning.[9]

For Further Reading

Dallas Willard, *Hearing God: Developing a Conversational Relationship with God* (Lisle, IL: InterVarsity Press, 2012), chapter 6, "The Word of God and the Rule of God," and chapter 7, "Redemption Through the Word of God."

Dallas Willard, "Transforming the Will," chapter 8 in *Renovation of the Heart: Putting on the Character of Christ* (Colorado Springs, CO: NavPress, 2002).

George Eldon Ladd, "The Mystery of the Kingdom," chapter 4 in *The Gospel of the Kingdom: Scriptural Studies in the Kingdom of God* (Grand Rapids, MI: Wm. B. Eerdmans, 1959).

David Wenham, *The Parables of Jesus* (Lisle, IL: InterVarsity Press, 1989), about the context and culture of the parables.

Notes

1. Dallas Willard, *The Great Omission: Reclaiming Jesus' Essential Teachings on Discipleship* (San Francisco: HarperOne, 2006), 155.
2. Portions of the analysis of the Parable of the Sower and the discussion of the human will in this chapter are drawn from the first nine minutes of Dallas Willard, "Understanding the Person 2," Atlanta Renovaré Institute video series, part 9, recorded October 2011 (this specific statement is at 3:31), https://conversatio.org/understanding-the-person-2.
3. C. S. Lewis, *The Screwtape Letters* (San Francisco: HarperSanFrancisco, 2001), 2–3.
4. Mother Teresa, *A Simple Path*, compiled by Lucinda Vardey (New York: Ballantine Books, 1995), 79, 94.
5. Dallas Willard, *Renovation of the Heart: Putting on the Character of Christ* (Colorado Springs, CO: NavPress, 2002), Kindle edition, 142.
6. Willard, *Hearing God*, 210.
7. Willard, *Hearing God*, 185.
8. Willard, *The Scandal of the Kingdom*, 42.
9. Willard, *Renovation of the Heart*, 29.

LESSON 4

THE SECRET INNER WORKING OF THE KINGDOM

Parables of the Growing Seed and the Mustard Seed (Mark 4:26–32)

God's Word is a substance that offers sustenance, just as food does. . . . We are learning how to live on the nourishment of the Word of God.

DALLAS WILLARD

Dallas Willard tells the story of how one time, as a university student, he was invited to teach the Bible in various places. It was then that he sensed God saying to him, "Never try to find a place to speak. Try to have something to say." Dallas believed that God taught him to concentrate on doing that: simply living his life with God and counting on him to have the outcome he wanted. This came as a source of relief, rest, and even empowerment to him.

We truly do not have to "make things happen," which can also be a source of relief to us as we interact in our work, our congregations, and our neighborhoods. Our role is to participate in the kingdom, to make disciples by being one, and to share what we have experienced. We don't have to push, convince, or "wow" people. We just let the living water of the Spirit flow and concentrate on taking it in. In this, we see that we don't have to try to get anyone to do anything—that is not our business. The Spirit does the "heavy lifting," so to speak.

This means that we can relax! In the Gospels, we find that Jesus was one of the most relaxed people who ever lived. He had complete confidence in the power of the Word that he spoke. Like the farmer in the Parable of the Growing Seed, he abandoned it to the ground, which is the point of the parable. The amazing results of the enormous spread of Christianity matched Jesus' confident faith. This is another benefit of having the faith *of* Christ, which allowed him to trust completely in God's providence. Like Jesus, we abandon the seed to the ground and let it work.

In the Parable of the Growing Seed that we will explore in this lesson, the seed is the focal point, not the farmer. All the farmer does is toss the seed onto the ground. The farmer has no idea how it grows—it just does. The farmer doesn't sit up all night hoping the seed will grow, checking it every ten minutes. He knows that the seed has a substance all its own, with its own agenda, producing a power all its own. In the same way, the "seed" of the Word of God is planted in people's hearts, and we don't have to try to make things happen.

1. When are some times that you have been tempted to "wow" other people with your acts of service or faith? What were the results of those attempts?

2. Do you ever feel pressured to say "just the right thing" out of fear that saying something wrong might turn someone away from the gospel? What do you think would be the result if you took a more relaxed approach and just let God work through you?

Hearing What Jesus Said

Maybe you have a friend who says surprising things that you can't quite forget. Jesus was that way. He thought "out of the box." No one in his day would have thought the kingdom of God was anything like a tiny, ordinary seed any more than we would say it is like a soda bottle. This technique of startling people made the truth more tangible and more easily remembered.

Jesus particularly liked to use the example of an everyday seed to describe the kingdom of God. As you read the following parable, in which the "growing seed" is the Word of God, recall from lesson 3 that the Word of God is God speaking—the thought and mind of God being expressed. It can refer to Jesus (the living Word), the Bible (the written Word), creation as an expression of God's thoughts and words, or the preaching and passing on of the Word of God.

> "The kingdom of God is as if a man should scatter seed on the ground, and should sleep by night and rise by day, and the seed should sprout and grow, he himself does not know how. For the earth yields crops by itself: first the blade, then the head, after that the full grain in the head. But when the grain ripens, immediately he [that is, the farmer—the man who is looking after his crop] puts in the sickle, because the harvest has come" (Mark 4:26–29 NKJV).

The kingdom of God is like the seed that was simply scattered by the farmer out on the ground. Jesus didn't say the farmer "planted" the seed. He just threw out the seeds as someone might let a tomato slip from a sandwich to the ground and then be surprised to find a tomato plant growing there in the spring. The farmer did nothing to cultivate it. In fact, "he himself [did] not know how" the seed sprouted and grew into a plant.

> Then He said, "To what shall we liken the kingdom of God? Or with what parable shall we picture it? It is like a mustard seed which, when it is sown on the ground, is smaller than all the seeds on earth; but when it is sown, it grows up and becomes greater than all herbs, and shoots out large branches, so that the birds of the air may nest under its shade" (Mark 4:30–32 NKJV).

Jesus made a point in this parable of saying that the mustard seed—the smallest of seeds—took root and grew into a bush big enough for birds to land in it, build nests in its branches, and hatch baby birds in it. Jesus used this to illustrate that the kingdom is not a certain time or place but a kind of life that keeps growing like the mustard seed. It grows far beyond the church into all areas of life—in business, in science, and in the arts.

In both the Parable of the Growing Seed and the Parable of the Mustard Seed, something of significant size grew out of an insignificant object, which would have filled any onlooker with surprise. The kingdom of God is the same way—small groups of people meeting here and there, but their love having a great impact on the people around them.

3. We get the impression that the farmer was puzzled and found the growth of the seed unexplainable. When have you seen that happen? (For example, a teenager comes home from church camp with a new sense of the presence of Christ, or a person who reluctantly came to church with you gets more out of the sermon than you did!)

4. Where have you seen evidence of the kingdom in surprising places? (For example, maybe a line from a movie or words that came out of the mouth of a teenager.)

Thinking About What Jesus Said

The Word: Power to Organize Reality

Nothing appears more often in Jesus' parables than seeds. They are tiny and inconspicuous, yet a few months later, they turn into lush grass or beautiful flowers or yummy things to eat. A seed is a dry little thing, maybe no bigger than your little fingernail. But put that in the ground, and soon a plant springs out of the earth. You water it and fertilize it, and after a little while you see a marvelous thing—maybe a watermelon—has emerged out of that little seed!

When you put that little seed into the earth, it's already packed with potent substances. There is enough power contained within a seed to crack its shell and put out a root. The seed knows exactly what it's supposed to absorb from the soil and what to leave behind. If it didn't know to select the right nutrients, it wouldn't function and would die. Its root has everything it takes to start eating dirt, eventually putting out a little leaf, then more leaves, and then fruit.

The seed thus organizes dirt, water, and sunlight to produce tasty food and beautiful plants. In this way, the seed has the power to organize reality. This is why the Word of God is portrayed as a seed. It also has the power to arrange processes and outcomes.

As we absorb the Word of God, we see into a deeper reality of how things are in the universe—how they really are with the people we love and the things we do. Just as God "sent His word and healed [Israel], and delivered them from their destructions" (Psalm 107:20 NKJV), so God offers us healing and moves us forward in the reality of the kingdom here and now. The Word has the power to reorganize our distorted thoughts and confused feelings so that we make good choices that amaze us: *What? I did that?*

The mustard seed, which Jesus emphasized was "the smallest of all seeds on earth" (Mark 4:31), in many ways resembled his ministry in Galilee, which was not near the important city of Jerusalem. Our ministry might likewise seem small and inconsequential: loving a cranky relative, paying attention to someone in our neighborhood, calling someone who is sick. Yet even such small "seeds" are bursting with unexpected power!

5. Find a seed, any seed. It can even be a sesame seed on your bagel or a pumpkin seed in your trail mix. Notice how small it is. Take a moment to wonder how it could possibly crack open, "eat dirt," and turn into something as large as a pumpkin. (If you wish, cut it in half and notice the contents.) Once you've done this, consider the Word of God as a small seed within you. Write down whatever comes to you as a prayer to God.

6. When has a specific insight from the Lord (or the Word of God) helped you to readjust, rethink, and transform your thinking or your views about people or circumstances?

God's Power at Work Through His Word

The Word of God is a *power* in this world. The Bible contains many eloquent descriptions of this power at work. Psalm 107 is one record of how God acted on Israel's behalf, sending his Word:

> And because of their iniquities, were afflicted. . . .
> Then they cried out to the LORD in their trouble,
> And He saved them out of their distresses.
> He *sent His word* and healed them,
> And delivered them from their destructions (Psalm 107:17, 19–20 NKJV, emphasis added).

Because the Word of God is living, it knows what it is doing. It is *purposive*. When "He sent His word and healed them," God was speaking in his kingdom. What distinguished the Word of Christ from others' teaching was that it was the Word of God. People were astonished that Jesus' words and doctrine came with power, saying that they had never heard anything like it before (see Luke 4:32). They tried to figure it out: "What is this? A new teaching—and with authority! He even gives orders to impure spirits and they obey him" (Mark 1:27). God had done it again: he *sent his Word*, and he healed them.

The psalmist saw all the phenomena of nature as obeying the Word of God:

> He sends out *His command* to the earth;
> *His word* runs very swiftly.
> He gives snow like wool;
> He scatters the frost like ashes . . .
> He sends out *His word* and melts them . . .
> He declares *His word* to Jacob,
> His statutes and *His judgments* to Israel (Psalm 147:15–16, 18, 19 NKJV, emphasis added).
>
> Fire and hail, snow and clouds; stormy wind, *fulfilling His word* (Psalm 148:8 NKJV, emphasis added).

In addition, the "implanted" Word is embedded and launched in us. We are to "humbly accept the word planted in [us], which can save [us]" (James 1:21). The implanted Word is like a seed because it is a power to organize reality. It will take what is in our lives and rearrange it.

Perhaps you have experienced the power of some people's words to make their listeners cringe in fear. But God's Word is a powerful vehicle to heal and to transform people (rearrange their lives). In God's hands and words, *power* is something that inspires you and make you want to partner with him, not something that causes you to fear.

7. When, if ever, have you experienced the power of nature in such a way that it seemed as if God were "speaking" through it? What was that experience like for you?

8. What does it mean to "humbly accept the word planted in you"? (Other translations say, "welcome with meekness the implanted word" [NRSVUE].)

The Gospel of Trying Too Hard

After reading a terrific book or hearing a stirring sermon, it can feel as if we need to do "just one more thing" in our life with God. It may be one more kind of prayer or one more type of service. Just one more! It may seem as if it is all up to us to make things happen.

However, while it is certainly true that there are things for us to do, we do them in cooperation with God and with the empowerment of the grace of God. Grace is God acting in our life to accomplish what we cannot do on our own. It infuses our being and our actions, making us more effective in the wisdom and power of God.

Dallas Willard once told about how, as a child, he tried to make a rosebud open. As he did so, it simply lay in his hand, a disarray of disjointed petals. In the same way, if we dig up a seed to see if the root is growing and then put it back in the ground, it will never grow. This is what often happens when we try to force things to happen instead of relying on God. We have to abandon the "seed" to the ground and leave it there.

Some people want nothing to do with Christ or the church because they've had their soul torn apart by well-intended Christians who pressured them to comply with what they thought it meant to be a Christian. Their souls have been wounded, as Paul said, because those well-intended Christians were zealous for God but their enthusiasm was not based on knowledge (see Romans 10:2). Paul had once been this kind of person who forced compliance. Our enthusiasm must be infused with patience as we wait for the seed to bear fruit.

Remember that time passed after the farmer scattered his seeds until a little shoot came out of the ground. He watched the plant as it grew, living each day as he normally did, and eventually there was something edible there. In the same way, we don't have to carry the load of making things happen. We just speak the Word of the gospel, live as a disciple of Jesus, lovingly teach, and be with people—and the growth will come.

9. What helps you to approach and complete your to-do list for the day not out of drudgery but in pleasant cooperation with and empowered by the Holy Spirit?

10. What sort of humility is required to no longer feel that you must make things happen?

Responding to What Jesus Said

Gentleness and Respect

The act of planting seeds in these and other parables is generally associated with sharing the Christian faith. Many people have been made to feel guilty for not speaking more forcefully to others about what they believe, but it is not our business to get people to think and say certain things. We are told to be a witness, but a witness doesn't try to convince anybody of anything.

Witnesses simply *say what they have seen and experienced* with the Word of truth to let the kingdom of God show in their lives and in their prayers. Witnesses are gracious, simply giving a reason for the hope that is within them with gentleness and respect (see 1 Peter 3:15). They can do these things with complete confidence that the seeds they plant will not be in vain.

Instead of trying to compel people into the kingdom, we do as the farmer did. He sowed the seed and then let it do its work. We also lay the seed down, whether it's what we say to our child or to a class we teach, and then choose to not be anxious about it. We recognize that being anxious about getting people to think a certain way or do a certain thing doesn't reflect Jesus' relaxed way of relying on the power of God. In fact, strained efforts to get people to do things makes it difficult for them to truly hear the Word of God. We give *God* the time to work.

As the Word dwells richly in our hearts and lives, we will find that we need fewer words to say the important things. We let our life speak. As hopeful and joyful people, we do things without complaining or arguing, shining as lights in the world (see Philippians 2:14–15).

11. In 1 Peter 3:15, we are instructed to talk about faith with *gentleness* and *respect.* What two words would you hope people would use to describe how you talk about your faith?

12. Take a few moments to read aloud the following poem by Teilhard de Chardin (a French Jesuit, Catholic priest, and theologian)—but do it slowly!

Patient Trust
Above all, trust in the slow work of God.
We are quite naturally impatient in everything
    to reach the end without delay.
We should like to skip the intermediate stages.
We are impatient of being on the way to do something
unknown,
    something new. . . .
Give Our Lord the benefit of believing
    that his hand is leading you.[1]

How do you sense today that God's hand is leading you in your life? Record your reflections below.

Key Term

Grace: God acting to accomplish what we cannot accomplish on our own. Grace is both active and passive—we receive it from God (passive) and it empowers us to move forward (active). We find both these forms in 1 Corinthians 15:10: "By the grace of God I am what I am, and his grace to me was not without effect. No, I worked harder than all of them—yet not I, but the grace of God that was with me." As Dallas Willard noted, grace is "a presence and power in life, which provides an alternative to the merely natural forces (flesh) accessible to the individual in and through the body without any specific divine intervention from above."[2]

For Further Reading

Dallas Willard, *Hearing God: Developing a Conversational Relationship with God* (Lisle, IL: InterVarsity Press, 2012), chapter 6, "The Word of God and the Rule of God," and chapter 7, "Redemption Through the Word of God."

George Eldon Ladd, "The Mystery of the Kingdom," chapter 4 in *The Gospel of the Kingdom: Scriptural Studies in the Kingdom of God* (Grand Rapids, MI: Wm. B. Eerdmans, 1959).

David Wenham, *The Parables of Jesus* (Lisle, IL: InterVarsity Press, 1989), about the context and culture of the parables.

Notes

1. "Prayer of Teilhard de Chardin," IgnatianSpirituality, accessed June 15, 2024, https://www.ignatianspirituality.com/prayer-of-theilhard-de-chardin/.
2. Willard, *Renovation of the Heart*, Kindle edition, 164.

LESSON 5

THE GREATEST OPPORTUNITY

Parables of the Wedding Feast, the Treasure in the Field, and the Pearl of Great Price (Luke 14:16–24; Matthew 13:44–46)

Discipleship to Jesus is the greatest opportunity we will ever have in life.

DALLAS WILLARD

Being a disciple of Jesus is the greatest opportunity that life here on earth offers to us. As disciples, we learn to live as Jesus taught us to live, which means we discover how to handle the ordinary events of daily life in cooperative action with God. We grow in learning how to act in God's power, not our own. As disciples, we also ask ourselves (and Jesus!), *How would he live our lives if he were us—in our vocations, our relationships, our health, our work, our leisure?* It is a continuing relationship through which all dimensions of our personality come to love God: mind, feelings, will (heart), body, social context, and soul.

Discipleship to Jesus is not miserable! Everything he commanded us to do is good for us and brings a good return to us. Yes, there are things we have to give up, but we become like the seeker in the Parable of the Treasure in the Field and the Parable of the Pearl of Great Price that we will explore in this lesson. We become eager to sell off or let go of nearly everything we own because we have found the gem we have been looking for our entire lives. We put all our energy into getting it and then we benefit immensely from the decision.

Jesus told us to "count the cost" of being his disciple (Luke 14:28 NKJV). In doing so, we not only look at what we *pay*; we also gaze on what we *gain*. We also need to count the cost of *not* being Jesus' disciple, for the cost of not doing something is often greater. For example, we may not know how much a new car is going to cost us until we also count up the cost of not buying it: bus fare, asking people for rides, and long walks home at night. Consider that avoiding discipleship might have a higher cost, including the likelihood of spending the rest of life being dominated by resentment and cynicism and by chasing satisfaction but finding none. Discipleship instead allows us to live a life full of love, joy, hope, peace, and confidence in God.

Many people who profess to know Christ have not intentionally *chosen* to be his disciples. It may be that no one ever presented that this is what Jesus had in mind in the Great Commission. Notice that Jesus said, "Go therefore and make disciples of all nations" (Matthew 28:19 NRSVUE), not "make Christians" or "make other church members."

Jesus went on to describe what these disciples should be:

- immersed in the Trinitarian life ("baptizing them in the name of the Father and of the Son and of the Holy Spirit," verse 19 NRSVUE);
- learning to live a surrendered life of obedience to Christ ("teaching them to obey everything that I have commanded you," verse 20 NRSVUE); and
- living constantly in the presence of Jesus ("And remember, I am with you always, to the end of the age," verse 20 NRSVUE).

The "feast" that awaits us—as revealed in the Parable of the Wedding Feast that we will also explore in this lesson—awaits us if we have said, "I will be a disciple of Jesus on *his* terms."

1. If you were to talk with someone who said he or she wanted to "start going to church" or "accept Christ" but thought being a disciple of Jesus was a bit much, what ideas might you set in front of that person? (Here are some ideas to get you started: It is more painful to "sit on the fence" than to climb down to either side; discipleship involves the riches of life with God—love, joy, hope, peace—instead of the guilt and doubt of trying to choose between God and everything that the world sets in front of you.)

2. Look at the descriptions of a disciple: (1) immersed in the Trinitarian life, (2) learning to live a surrendered life of obedience to Christ, and (3) living constantly in the presence of Jesus. Which stands out to you as one you *really* want for yourself? (If you're willing, read each aloud. Then close your eyes to answer the question. See what comes to you.)

Hearing What Jesus Said

As Jesus spoke to the crowds, he no doubt saw the faces of people who were challenged to be his disciples but weren't yet able to follow. So he offered them this picture:

"A certain man gave a great supper and invited many, and sent his servant at supper time to say to those who were invited, 'Come, for all things are now ready.' But they all with one accord began to make excuses. The first said to him, 'I have bought a piece of ground, and I must go and see it. I ask you to have me excused.' And another said, 'I have bought five yoke of oxen, and I am going to test them. I ask you to have me excused.' Still another said, 'I have married a wife, and therefore I cannot come.' So that servant came and reported these things to his master. Then the master of the house, being angry, said to his servant, 'Go out quickly into the streets and lanes of the city, and bring in here the poor and the maimed and the lame and the blind.' And the servant said, 'Master, it is done as you commanded, and still there is room.' Then the master said to the servant, 'Go out into the highways and hedges, and compel them to come in, that my house may be filled. For I say to you that none of those men who were invited shall taste my supper'" (Luke 14:16–24 NKJV).

A formal supper in Jesus' day lasted a long time—perhaps a few days. Notice that the people who declined to attend this great event had received the invitation some time before and had either agreed to come or had given no indication they were not coming. Notice also the illogical nature of the excuses that each of the guests gave for not coming. The first man's excuse of having to see land that he had purchased makes you wonder why he didn't see the land *before* he bought it. The story of the guest who wanted to test the oxen he had bought also doesn't add up—anyone would test oxen *before* buying them. Still another man offered the excuse of having gotten married . . . but why couldn't he just bring his wife with him?

All these folks offered obstacles that were so illogical they were probably not true. It appears they had something else they wanted to do that was more important to them but didn't want to say what it was. What we see above all is that they didn't care about the person who was inviting them. This should lead us to ask, "Do we love God and his kingdom?" It may be that we haven't been taught enough about life in the kingdom of God to answer this question with a yes or a no. So, to make it simpler, we could ask, "Do we love the kind of day-by-day interaction with God that we see in the life of Jesus, in the early church, and perhaps have experienced in our own lives?" God will not force the kingdom down our throat.

3. Notice that the host didn't push the dinner guests to attend the great supper by offering bribes, flattery, gimmicks, shame, coercion, or "come and get it" strategies. What does this say about how we should approach others in conversations about knowing Christ? What does it say about how followers of Jesus should approach evangelism?

4. The excuses that were offered by those who declined the banquet invitation involved work situations (fields, oxen) and relationships (marriage). However, God doesn't ask us to give up these things or minimize them. So what does discipleship to Jesus look like in relation to making a living and cultivating relationships?

Thinking About What Jesus Said

Pursuers of the Great Opportunity

People of faith often do not comprehend the greatness of the invitation to life in the kingdom of God. The apostle Paul described it as "the *unsearchable* riches of

Christ" (Ephesians 3:8 NKJV, emphasis added). Other translations use words such as *unfathomable*, *incalculable*, *incomprehensible*, and *inexhaustible*. If we can't fathom something, it means we never reach the bottom of it. No matter how far we go, there is still more!

Jesus understood that in our finite, self-focused way, we don't comprehend how great an opportunity it is to live as a disciple in the kingdom of God in the here and now. So he drew more pictures to illustrate this opportunity with two other parables:

> "Again, the kingdom of heaven is like treasure hidden in a field, which a man found and hid; and for joy over it he goes and sells all that he has and buys that field" (Matthew 13:44 NKJV).

Imagine someone hired to dig in a field who suddenly finds treasure—maybe oil or gold. He sells all his resources to buy the field, thinking it is the best opportunity ever presented. He is ready to do whatever he can to possess it because he understands it to be an investment.

> "Again, the kingdom of heaven is like a merchant seeking beautiful pearls, who, when he had found one pearl of great price, went and sold all that he had and bought it" (Matthew 13:45–46 NKJV).

The pearl merchant in this parable had the wisdom to detect the transcendent value of the gem. So, with excitement and joy, he sold all his other pearls and all his other resources so that he could buy that one pearl. He didn't regret this decision later because he knew this pearl was worth everything he had. He was glad to give up those other things.

Once we understand who Jesus is and what knowing him means for our lives, we realize that discipleship to him is the greatest opportunity we will ever have. We gain perspective about the many good things in our lives and eventually choose to give them up in order to gain possession of the priceless treasure of the kingdom of God. It's no sacrifice to us at all.

If we present Christ correctly, the effect will be to ravish people with the reality of the kingdom. They will think that they have nothing better to do! That's how you make disciples.

5. When the person digging in the field saw the treasure, he thought of all the things that would be possible for him if he were able to possess that treasure. Think of the possibilities of a life lived trusting God—a life lived in the presence of Christ with the guidance and power of the Holy Spirit. Here are some ideas to get you started:

grateful	instead of...	self-pitying
forgiving	instead of...	resentful
being a giver	instead of...	being a taker
self-sacrificing	instead of...	self-indulgent
God-confident	instead of...	self-loathing

What are some of the possibilities that you see specifically in your life?

6. Many field-workers would have walked away from the treasure or been suspicious of it. Or perhaps they would have tried to buy the field but found it impossible to obtain. Likewise, many pearl merchants would have passed or given up on the opportunity to own the nearly priceless pearl. Given this, what good qualities were present in the people featured in these two parables? Name as many as you can.

Seeing the Greatness of God

In his book *Your God Is Too Small,* author and Anglican clergyman J. B. Phillips wrote about the problem of not grasping the greatness of God and the magnificence of Christ in the Gospels. He notes that when Christians talk about Jesus, they often see an idealistic or powerless person who doesn't compare well with others. Here are a few of his "too small" versions of God:

- **Resident policeman:** someone who stalks you to see what you are doing wrong.
- **Parental hangover:** someone who possesses all the faults of your parents but none of their good points.
- **Grand old man:** a distant and perhaps senile individual who pats you on the back and has little interest in your real life.
- **Meek and mild:** someone who has little to say, who is not adventurous or courageous, and who is not even interesting.
- **Pale Galilean:** this person floats through a field of flowers carrying a lamb.[1]

All these versions overlook the adventurous and courageous Jesus who spoke to gale-force winds (and they obeyed!) and worked hard as a carpenter in Galilee—meaning that he would have dealt with royal officials as well as slaves of Rome who were building Herod's nearby palace in Tiberias.[2] These views also overlook how Jesus protected his disciples and stood up to the powerful religious leaders of his day as well as the Roman officials.

Dallas Willard noted that when university students occasionally asked him, "Why are you a disciple of Jesus?" he usually replied, "Who else did you have in mind?" He wasn't being flip in his response; he meant it seriously. The students wanted to tell him how great Buddha, Gandhi, or even their favorite musician, politician, or athlete was, but Dallas calmly said that upon close examination, *none* of them compared to Christ.

The reality is that we are all "following" somebody who is good at something. We follow a person in acquiring wealth, or being the best possible parent, or looking good in our older years. Some questions for us to ask are, *Who are we really following? Who do we look up to? Who are our role models?* No matter who that person might be, we need to recognize that this person's goodness is finite. However, the goodness of God that is available through following Jesus is so unfathomable that we will never see the end of it!

7. Take a few minutes in a quiet place to ask God to show you who you are following. It might be a parent you admire or a made-up person who is the opposite of a parent you don't admire. It could be a character in a movie or someone described in a self-help book. Ask, *Who am I really following? Who do I look up to? Who are my role models?* Write down your responses to what God reveals to you in the space below.

8. Take ten to fifteen minutes to sit in a beautiful space. Read aloud Psalm 145 and put emphasis on the word *all*, which occurs sixteen times in the New International Version. Which idea about God do you find most fascinating in this psalm? Why?

Discipleship Will Look Odd

One of the most perplexing statements that Jesus made to the crowds who were following him was, "If anyone comes to me and does not hate father and mother, wife and children, brothers and sisters—yes, even their own life—such a person cannot be my disciple. And whoever does not carry their cross and follow me cannot be my disciple" (Luke 14:26–27).

Jesus was not saying, "I won't *let* this person be my disciple." He was saying this person *could not* be his disciple. This person was *unable* to be Jesus' disciple because all his thoughts were centered on the welfare of his family and himself. This is simple logic, much like saying, "If you can't reach up more than five feet, you can't grab something on a shelf at a height of seven feet." No one is going *stop* the person from trying to reach that shelf. He simply *won't* be able to reach it because he is not tall enough. Likewise, those who are unable to focus on Christ and consult God in prayer will find that they are unable to be a disciple of Jesus in all of life.

We need an *inward* attitude that is willing to set aside all we have, including whatever wealth we possess and whatever relationships we treasure. As disciples, we honor those relationships and act as good stewards of our possessions, but those things are not uppermost in our minds. In regard to them, we stay in constant thought of God's desire for us to use such objects rightly and treat those we love with reverence, respect, and patience (which may not be the first thing that comes to mind). Only with the guidance of the Spirit can we seek *first* the kingdom of God and his deep goodness in everything we do.

Now, in doing these things, it is likely that we will look odd to others. Just imagine how bad it looked when James and John left their father, Zebedee, in the boat with his hired men because they wanted to follow Jesus (Mark 1:19–20). Zebedee had a good business. Perhaps he thought, *My sons must hate me to do this to me!* No doubt others thought that too.

So, when you choose to be a disciple of Jesus, expect that people will find you to be odd at times. They might be surprised that you don't prize your possessions or seek to boost your reputation like the rest of the world. They might be shocked at the extent of your financial giving or that you forgive people for the outrageous things that they have done to you. Know in all this that it's okay when others consider you to be odd for being a disciple of Jesus, because you are partnering with the Creator of the universe to bring goodness and love to the world.

9. It's not necessarily that relationships and possessions are obstacles in following God, but your viewpoint of them certainly can be. How would you describe that viewpoint?

10. How do you respond to the idea that others might find it odd when you choose to be a disciple of Christ? What helps you to care as much or more about what *God* thinks of you as opposed to what *other people* think of you?

Responding to What Jesus Said

Jesus the Mentor

If you want someone to be your mentor, it is likely that you admire the skills that person has. However, it is even more likely that you desire to be like that person as it relates to his or her personality and character. You think to yourself, *This is someone I don't want to miss out on knowing! I want this person's input in my life decisions.*

The same is true of Jesus. Just think about some of the admirable personality traits that he possessed. For instance, he was able to travel with twelve men who held opposing political viewpoints and had differing vocations. This group didn't splinter in spite of their differences but stayed together and looked to Christ to answer their questions. Jesus was also able to remain calm in the presence of his accusers. When the soldiers came to arrest him in the garden of Gethsemane, he calmly told them that he was the one they were looking for. He protected his disciples, saying, "If you are looking for me, then let these men go" (John 18:8).

Jesus invited *all* to follow him. God chose each of us in Christ long ago. Paul tells us, "Long before he laid down earth's foundations, he had us in mind, had settled on us as the focus of his love, to be made whole and holy by his love" (Ephesians 1:4 MSG). God sees us as family and wants us to be part of his family business. We are made to create good and love others, not to simply watch sitcoms and play solitaire. A life with Jesus gives us the things we want most: to be truly seen, truly heard, truly wanted, and have a bit of adventure in the mix.

Jesus is the wisest of mentors. You might be surprised to discover how he will help you handle all kinds of situations and make the right decisions when you *ask him for his input and are attentive enough to hear what he has to say*. Go ahead and try it!

11. Consider the range of Jesus' actions. He told good stories to help people understand (see Mark 4:33) but also walked through a crowd getting ready to throw him off a cliff (see Luke 4:29–30). He was patient enough to heal all the sick in one town in one night (see Matthew 8:16) but also showed himself the "master of the house" in cleansing the temple (see Mark 11:15). What traits do you most admire in Jesus? Why those traits?

12. Have an honest conversation with Jesus. Picture the two of you sitting together on a park bench and just chatting with each other. Do you truly want to be a disciple? If not, why not—or what is your hesitation? If so, ask Jesus, "What is my next step?"

Key Term

Discipleship: The process through which all dimensions of one's personality come to the love of God. Discipleship is a continuing relationship relating to one's whole life, not just religion. There are three main aspects of it: (1) learning to do as Jesus did and as he taught, (2) learning to handle the events of daily life in cooperative action with God, and (3) learning how to act in God's power, whether that is operating a business, fixing a machine, helping a child, or whatever else. A person learns discipleship by living interactively with Jesus' resurrected presence (through his Word, his personal presence, and through other people) as he or she progressively learns *to lead his or her life as Jesus would if he were in that person's place.*[3]

For Further Reading

Dallas Willard, *The Great Omission: Reclaiming Jesus' Essential Teachings on Discipleship* (San Francisco: HarperOne, 2006), chapters 1–5, on discipleship.

Kenneth Bailey, *Jesus Through Middle Eastern Eyes: Cultural Studies in the Gospels* (Lisle, IL: InterVarsity Press, 2008), chapter 24.

J. B. Phillips, *Your God Is Too Small: A Guide for Believers and Skeptics Alike* (New York: Touchstone, 2004).

John Bowen, *The Unfolding Gospel: How the Good News Makes Sense of Discipleship, Church, Mission, and Everything Else* (Minneapolis, MN: Fortress Press, 2021), about the gospel and discipleship.

Notes

1. J. B. Phillips, *Your God Is Too Small* (New York: Touchstone, 2004), 5.
2. Richard A. Batey, *Jesus and the Forgotten City* (Grand Rapids, MI: Baker, 1991), 70.
3. Willard, *The Great Omission*, 166.

LESSON 6

GROWING TOGETHER IN THE KINGDOM

Parable of the Weeds and the Wheat (Matthew 13:24–30, 37–43)

We must be careful about judging others.

DALLAS WILLARD

God's invitation to enter his kingdom is broad and inclusive. He is eager for all to enter and is patient with people, not wanting to lose anyone but desiring to see everyone choose to seek him (see 2 Peter 3:9). In the Parable of the Wedding Feast that we explored in the last lesson, we saw how God expanded this invitation when those who were initially invited did not come. The host told his servants to go out into the country roads and the city streets and bring in anybody (see Luke 14:23). The host didn't put qualifications on them in any way.

Given the nature of God's open invitation, our churches often have a mixture of people with varying motives growing together. In the parable that we will discuss in this lesson, Jesus pictured this phenomenon as a field filled with both wheat and weeds. Because the kingdom of God is available to all, there are weak and needy people who will be interested in joining. This may cause irritations to some, but we can trust that this is part of God's plan. Instead of judging each other, we keep making disciples in the church and in our communities as others experience us as the salt and light of Jesus in our workplaces and neighborhoods. As more disciples gather to form a church, we live into a shared identification with Christ, making it possible for our communities of faith to become a positive reality at which others marvel.

According to Jesus, our primary responsibility is to help people come to know him—specifically, to *make disciples*—not test them to determine their fitness or sincerity. God's open invitation means that any kingdom gathering, even a church, will include people of widely different tastes in music, dress, and ways of speaking. There may even be a wide divergence on doctrine. When it comes to mistakes in doctrine, as Dallas Willard used to say, "It's not like someone will miss heaven by five points." He also noted that no doubt *all of us* are a bit cloudy on some doctrine, even though we may have read books on the subject and spent much time in study.

The possibility of judgment among followers of Christ, whether vocalized or not, is always there. However, we have to remember that Jesus came into this world not to be served but to serve (see Mark 10:45). He likewise calls us not to *judge* others but to *serve* others: "Do not judge, or you too will be judged. For in the same way you judge others, you will be judged, and with the measure you use, it will be measured to you" (Matthew 7:1–2). As Jude adds, "Go easy on those who hesitate in the faith. Go after those who take the wrong way. Be tender with sinners, but not soft on sin. The sin itself stinks to high heaven" (1:22–23 MSG).

1. Why do you think Jesus thought it was a good idea to invite anybody (both the "wheat" and the "weeds") to come into God's kingdom?

2. When it comes to the "troublesome" people in the church, you always have the choice in judging them or moving them toward becoming disciples of Jesus. Which would you say that you tend to do the most? What would it take for you to more consistently approach people with an attitude of serving them rather than judging them?

Hearing What Jesus Said

Certain types of grass known as "cheat" look like oats, but they are actually weeds that can take over a plot of land. In the Parable of the Wheat and the Weeds, the owner of a field had a similar problem with weeds masquerading as wheat:

> Jesus told them another parable: "The kingdom of heaven is like a man who sowed good seed in his field. But while everyone was sleeping, his enemy came and sowed weeds among the wheat, and went away. When the wheat sprouted and formed heads, then the weeds also appeared.
>
> "The owner's servants came to him and said, 'Sir, didn't you sow good seed in your field? Where then did the weeds come from?'
>
> " 'An enemy did this,' he replied.
>
> "The servants asked him, 'Do you want us to go and pull them up?'
>
> " 'No,' he answered, 'because while you are pulling the weeds, you may uproot the wheat with them. Let both grow together until the harvest. At that time I will tell the harvesters: First collect the weeds and tie them in bundles to be burned; then gather the wheat and bring it into my barn' " (Matthew 13:24–30).

Some people get a great sense of accomplishment by pulling weeds out of their garden. But in a field of wheat and weeds, you can't do that because it's not always possible to skillfully distinguish one from the other or separate them. You might pull up what you think are weeds during the growing season only to find that you have destroyed some of the wheat. But at harvest time when the wheat has matured, it's easy to detect the wheat from the weeds.

After the crowds had left and the disciples were alone with Jesus, they requested clarification about this parable. Jesus replied:

> "The one who sowed the good seed is the Son of Man. The field is the world, and the good seed stands for the people of the kingdom. The weeds are the people of the evil one, and the enemy who sows them is the devil. The harvest is the end of the age, and the harvesters are angels.
>
> "As the weeds are pulled up and burned in the fire, so it will be at the end of the age. The Son of Man will send out his angels, and they will weed out of his kingdom everything that causes sin and all who do evil. They will throw them into the blazing furnace, where there will be weeping and gnashing of teeth. Then the righteous will shine like the sun in the kingdom of their Father. Whoever has ears, let them hear" (Matthew 13:37–43).

In this parable, the field is the world (not the church) and the seeds are described as "people of the kingdom" who have either received the Word of God and are maturing or are "people of the evil one" who are still of the world, which is "under the control of the evil one" (1 John 5:19). In scriptural language, "children of" refers to those resembling someone above them. Some people will resemble the kingdom and its God-centered ways and others will resemble the wicked one and its self-focused ways.

Once again, the inclusiveness of the kingdom invitation means there are people who are of the world (weeds) who need to receive the Word of God in their lives to become children of the kingdom. But weeds can become wheat through the power of God's Word.

3. Some people find this parable puzzling and are quick to condemn themselves or others as "weeds." How do you respond to this parable? What are your questions about it?

4. If you consider yourself a child of God, what would you most like to be (more) true of yourself so you would more closely resemble what God is like?

Thinking About What Jesus Said

Why God Allows Weeds

In the Parable of the Wedding Feast that we discussed in the last lesson, we saw that all kinds of people were invited into the kingdom and no one was excluded unless they refused to come (see Luke 14:23–24). In the Parable of the Weeds and the Wheat, we find that two different types of people have accepted the invitation: those who choose to live their lives of the kingdom (wheat) and those who choose not to be of the kingdom because their thoughts and actions do not resemble God (weeds). Both appear to be *in* the kingdom, but both are not *of* the kingdom. Those two small prepositions, *in* and *of*, create an important distinction.

What does it mean to be *of* something? *Of* refers to one's origin and nature (or character). You may see a child and say, "She is one of the Kims." This daughter, who originated from Mr. and Mrs. Kim, is likely to share the character and attitudes of her parents. No matter what circumstances she may be *in*, she is *of* the Kim family. The wheat in Jesus' parable represents those who, just like this daughter, are both *in* the kingdom and *of* the kingdom. Their origin is of the kingdom and they have a character that resembles their heavenly Father.

The weeds represent those who seem to be *in* God's kingdom but who are not *of* it because they "[cause] sin" and "do evil" (Matthew 13:41). They may be involved in kingdom activities, but their nature (character) remains of the world. They possess and cultivate thoughts and desires that come from the world and their nature is restricted to the world (see 1 John 2:19; 1 Corinthians 3–5). They may like the idea of having faith, might be churchgoers, and may have even seen people changed, but they think of the church as a *building* instead of a *people* who are infiltrating the whole world. Their "church life," or what they think of God, is restricted to being a "fairly good person" and even doing certain "church activities," but they have never interacted enough with God for it to penetrate their character.

It may seem strange, but it is possible for people to be *in* the reach of divine power but not be *of* that power. Jesus says of them, "The Son of Man will send out his angels, and they will weed out of his kingdom everything that causes sin and all who do evil" (Matthew 13:41).

5. Some people find it difficult that God allows the wheat and the weeds to grow together in the world until the harvest. They tend to agree with the servant who wanted to pull up the weeds. Why do you think God does this? How do you feel about it?

6. There are some people who have not engaged in enough interaction with God for it to penetrate their character. What are some of the traits of these kinds of people? What does this say about the importance of interacting with God on a daily basis?

Oasis in the Desert

Being *in* the world is not a bad thing; it's a good thing. The world is God's creation. We, like Jesus, interact with all kinds of people in this world—those who follow God and those who participate in less than desirable activities. Jesus was even criticized for associating with the latter (see Luke 15:1–2). When we mingle with those who are *of* the world, that doesn't mean that we are. Living for Christ means being *in* the world but not *of* the world. We live squarely in the world but with a Christlike character, offering a steady gleam of love, joy, and peace.

Picture this in terms of a desert with sand and dust as far as the eye can see. In the middle of that desert, a spring of water bubbles up, forming a pool of refreshment for all who happen by. We could say that the spring and the pool are *in* the desert but are not *of* it. They do not originate in the desert but come from the rains, streams, and snow on faraway mountains that travel through hidden passageways in the earth. The stream and the pool are not of the same nature as the desert and, in fact, they seem unnatural there.

You can likewise be *in* something without being *of* it. A person can be in a university without being an educated person. Someone can be in an art museum without being an artist. And someone can be in a church without being a disciple of Jesus. Being in something is a much more superficial thing than being of it.

Those who are truly *of* the kingdom of God have an origin and nature that comes from that kingdom. They have experienced the new birth that Jesus talked about with Nicodemus (see John 3:1–21). They are born of the Word of God, and that Word is the spiritual activity by which they are brought into the kingdom of God.

Like the wind, the Spirit comes and moves in the lives of individuals so they become of the kingdom of God. People see the results, but they can't see what has caused the results. This is abundant life in its fullest sense: one lived from hidden sources that come into the soul from God and his kingdom. Such abundant life is possible no matter where you are or what you happen to be doing.

7. Think of a time you have felt like a pool in the desert. What does it take to be okay with this experience to be *in* the world but clearly *of* God's kingdom?

8. How do you think Jesus was able to remain a godly presence with those who participated in "less than desirable" activities? (Don't just say he had a free ticket by being the Son of God! He was fully human, lured in every way we are.)

Receive People as They Are

If you are concerned about your standing in God's kingdom, you can be assured that if you are simply walking as a disciple of Christ, you are living in the reality of being both *in* the kingdom of God and *of* the kingdom of God. The apostle Paul wrote, "If the Spirit of him who raised Jesus from the dead is living in you, he who raised Christ from the dead will also give life to your mortal bodies" (Romans 8:11). The one who raised Christ from the dead can give life to your earthly body now as well as later. You can know that power if you choose to know it.

Disciples of Jesus include people at all stages of the journey with God—including those who might still be in captivity. God does not say, "Get ready, and then come into my kingdom." No, he just says, "Come into my kingdom." This openness and bigheartedness of the message brings people in, and as they come, we invite them to become disciples of Jesus.

The church is like a hospital with people at different stages of healing and health. Some are receiving treatment and improving. Some are in intensive care. Others are getting well and going out into the world with the soft radiance of "a better country" in their eyes (see Hebrews 11:16). It can be tempting to think of the people on your floor of the church-hospital as being fine but question "those people" on the other floors. Yet the truth is that the church is not a place of perfection but a place where people live with one another in healing love under the power of God. So we should expect and receive people as they are. That was Jesus' way.

It can be discouraging for us to know that weeds are growing among the wheat in our churches. It can be troubling to realize that some folks are there for the wrong reasons. However, as Paul wrote, our confidence is found in Christ, not in the competency or incompetency of others (see 2 Corinthians 3:4). It is out of the abundance of the confidence that we have in Christ that we act. We do not act out of scarcity, fear, or weakness. We act out of *his* strength, fullness, and confidence. And by doing that, we enter into a power that is so great that we can speak of the kingdom advancing among human beings.

9. The difference between being of the *kingdom* and of the *world* is more of a continuum. Where do you see yourself on the scale? (Talk to Jesus before you do this.)

Of the world — Of the kingdom

More importantly, why do you situate yourself in that place?

10. There are people who might profess to have great faith in Christ but their actions and attitudes make you uneasy. What does it mean to you that your confidence and strength is found in Christ and not others? What does it make you want to pray?

Responding to What Jesus Said

Discernment Versus Judgment

Remember that Jesus likened the kingdom of God to a mustard seed that grows into a huge tree supporting "the birds of the air" that find shelter and build nests there (Luke 13:19 ESV). Sometimes when we look at our church's fellowship, we may wonder how all those different kinds of birds have landed there! But this is what Jesus was saying in the Parable of the Weeds and the Wheat. It's not *wrong* that all those "birds" are there. It's what we should expect.

It's interesting that the servants in Jesus' parable asked the owner of the field, "Where then did the weeds come from? . . . Do you want us to go and pull them up?" (Matthew 13:27–28). We, like these servants, often ask the same about those whom we perceive to be "weeds." But God, like the owner, understood the relationships between people and the harm that would be caused if he allowed us to "pull them up." In Jesus' explanation, the harvesters are the *angels*, not us. We may discern defects of character and mixed motives in others, but we use that to inform our prayers for them, not to condemn them.

The English word *judge* encompasses two different ideas: discernment and condemnation. That term *discern* is important. Discernment involves wisdom and clarity and is open to change. Condemnation disapproves and even renounces a person. Such judgment may occur only in a person's mind or it may extend to gossip or formal censure. But with discernment, we learn to be "wise as serpents and harmless as doves" (Matthew 10:16 NKJV).

Our task is clear as followers of Jesus who are seeking to help others become disciples of Christ. We are to pray for them and to "consider how we may spur one another on toward love and good deeds" so that we are not "giving up meeting together, as some are in the habit of doing, but encouraging one another" (Hebrews 10:24–25).

11. Let's say you have a friend whom you know is secretly engaging in some kind of sin. What does discernment look like in that case? What does judgment look like in that case?

12. Try the following exercise to close out this lesson. Find a picture, contact page, or social media page of someone whom you are very tempted to judge. Gaze at it with two thoughts in mind: (1) God says that every person is made in his image (see Genesis 1:27), and (2) God says you are to honor others above yourself (see Romans 12:10). Ask God to fill you with discernment, wisdom, love, and kindness regarding this person. Write out your reflections below on what God revealed to you during this time.

Key Terms

***In* the world:** Interacting with people who are typical of the overriding culture "of the world" and embody a nature and character that is primarily self-focused.

***In* the kingdom:** Interacting with people who understand the culture "of God's kingdom" and understand his kingdom values to be right and good.

***Of* the kingdom:** Embodying the nature and character of God's kingdom: love, joy, peace, hope, and confidence in him. *Of* refers to one's origin and nature.

For Further Reading

Dallas Willard, *The Divine Conspiracy: Rediscovering Our Hidden Life in God* (New York: HarperCollins, 1998), chapter 5.

George Eldon Ladd, "The Mystery of the Kingdom," chapter 4 in *The Gospel of the Kingdom: Scriptural Studies in the Kingdom of God* (Grand Rapids, MI: Wm. B. Eerdmans, 1959).

Brant Hansen, *Unoffendable: How Just One Change Can Make All of Life Better* (Nashville, TN: W Publishing Group, 2015).

LESSON 7

GROWTH AND RESPONSIBILITY IN THE KINGDOM

Parable of the Talents (Luke 19:12–26)

Taking responsibility and investing in the future was a crucial part of the message of Jesus.

DALLAS WILLARD

Did you know that *you* have a kingdom? God intends for you to have a realm (an area of influence) where you "take charge" of certain things. God gave humanity dominion over everything on the earth when he created Adam and Eve (see Genesis 1:28), and he did not set that aside when they chose to disobey him in the Fall. Each of us *still* has the job of managing the earth and caring for it—and this works best under God's guidance.

Besides that, each of us has a say over certain things that happen in our sphere of influence, where things are done in the way we have decided they should be done. This includes our actions: the way we brush our teeth, how we drive a car, how we treat people, and how we fulfill the jobs we have undertaken. These things, over which we have some say, make up our "kingdom" or "queendom," so to speak. This is a realm that is uniquely our own, and however large or small that area of influence may be, God intends for us to step into it.

No one is without a kingdom or queendom—a domain over which they have the say. If you ever question whether this is true, just try to get in the way of someone when he or she is planning to do something. If you interfere, don't expect it to go well. You are encroaching on that person's kingdom, and he or she will not want you to do that. The fact that humans have a domain over which they have the say explains much of the conflict we see when kingdoms collide between individuals, within families, between social groups, and among nations.

When Jesus announced the availability of the kingdom of God, he also invited us to harmonize all our individual domains so that we could live together without antagonism. God did not intend our present kingdoms on earth to be in conflict with one another. Instead, we have the privilege and responsibility in our domains to say and do everything as Jesus would say and do them, with gratitude in our hearts to God (see Colossians 3:17).

The way this works out practically is that God expects us to take charge over the things around us with careful thought and intentionality. We do so in a manner that demonstrates that we love the Lord with our whole being and love our neighbor as ourselves (see Luke 10:27). Managing our money is a primary part of this responsibility because it extends the capacity of what we are able to accomplish in our domains. Jesus understood this fact—that money gives power to make things happen—and thus often spoke about money in his parables. He desires for us to learn how to act with initiative and use our time, possessions, and bodies *in reliance on him* to create the greatest good that we can for the glory of God.

1. How warm are you (or not) to the idea that every person on this earth has a domain over which he or she has the say? Explain your response.

2. What five things can you name that are in your "kingdom"? (Consider such things as your possessions, activities you choose to do, or the kind of person you want to be.)

Hearing What Jesus Said

The Parable of the Talents that Jesus told is not about the final judgment but about our responsibilities in contemporary life. Talents (or minas in the Luke 19 version) were a common unit of money in Jesus' day. So today, this story could be called the "Parable of the Dollar."

> "A certain nobleman went into a far country to receive for himself a kingdom and to return. So he called ten of his servants, delivered to them ten minas, and said to them, 'Do business till I come'" (Luke 19:12–13 NKJV).

It often happened at the time that a person would go to Rome and return having been made king over a territory. Before this man left, he gave ten servants one mina, which was worth roughly a hundred days' wages—almost four months' income. The servants were told to use the money, and the nobleman trusted their judgment about how to go about doing that.

> "And so it was that when he returned, having received the kingdom, he then commanded these servants, to whom he had given the money, to be called to him, that he might know how much every man had gained by trading. Then came the first, saying, 'Master, your mina has earned ten minas'" (Luke 19:15–16 NKJV).

The first servant had a 1,000 percent gain on the investment. His story reveals that we should be in conversation with God about how to use our initiative to promote the greatest amount of good for his kingdom. Such partnering builds our relationship with him.

> "And he said to him, 'Well done, good servant; because you were faithful in a very little, have authority over ten cities.' And the second came, saying, 'Master, your mina has earned five minas.' Likewise he said to him, 'You also be over five cities.'
>
> "Then another came, saying, 'Master, here is your mina, which I have kept put away in a handkerchief. For I feared you, because you are an austere man. You collect what you did not deposit, and reap what you did not sow.' And he said to him, 'Out of your own mouth I will judge you, you wicked servant. You knew that I was an austere man, collecting what I did not deposit and reaping what I did not sow. Why then did you not put my money in the bank, that at my coming I might have collected it with interest?'
>
> "And he said to those who stood by, 'Take the mina from him, and give it to him who has ten minas.' (But they said to him, 'Master, he has ten minas.') 'For I say to you, that to everyone who has will be given; and from him who does not have, even what he has will be taken away from him'" (Luke 19:17–26 NKJV).

In Matthew's account, the third servant said, "Lord, I knew you to be a hard man, reaping where you have not sown, and gathering where you have not scattered seed. And I was afraid, and went and hid your talent in the ground" (Matthew 25:24–25 NKJV). In each account, the servant exhibited the attitude of those who do not move forward in God's kingdom because they don't know how good and generous God is. They have not absorbed the truth of God's love and the dignity that he gave human beings at creation. We must take ourselves seriously as God's creatures, believing that we are worth his investment in us.

The master's words in Luke 19:26 may seem harsh at first glance: "I tell you that to everyone who has, more will be given, but from the one who has not, even what he has will be taken away" (ESV). But consider how this universal truth applies to weight lifting. Those who consistently lift weights can eventually lift more, while those who stop lifting weights find they can't lift what they previously did. Whatever you put your energy into will increase; whatever you ignore will decrease. The more readiness to receive from God a person has, the more they will receive. However, if a person is not receptive to God, what they have will diminish.

3. In what way did the third servant not regard himself as seriously as his master did?

4. What are some things you put your energy into and witnessed an increase? Or, what are some things you have neglected that you witnessed decrease?

Thinking About What Jesus Said

Taking Ourselves Seriously

Living in the kingdom of God involves taking responsibility for the kind of people we are becoming and what God has given to us. The problem with the third servant in the Parable of the Talents was that he did *nothing* with what the master had given to him—and thought that was a good idea! To do nothing in our life with God means there is no increase in our love for God, no spiritual growth, and no partnering in the expansion of his kingdom.

Taking responsibility in this way means being intentional about your life with God. It's not about outcomes; it's about following through in faith. Jeremiah and other Old Testament prophets were extremely faithful to God but didn't live to see Israel turn around. Still, they remained connected to God in spite of this fact. If we use what God has already given us (as they did), God will trust us with even more responsibility, knowledge, and character.

You may feel hesitant about taking the initiative in this because you question your abilities or are reluctant to trust God with them. If so, follow the example of Moses and ask God to help you. When Moses asked, the Lord gave him a helper (see Exodus 4:11–16). God works so quietly that you may not experience something extra happening, but often you will. Your everyday trust in God to help you will show up brilliantly when you look back on things.

For now, focus on taking responsibility for things uniquely your own, where your choice determines what happens. You can *practice* faith in the kingdom of God: see how it works, move with it, and know that it's real. God has extended the invitation to you. "You do it. You know I'm there, but you do it. And I'll act with you."

As you do this, remember that the important thing in God's kingdom is the kind of person you are becoming, not your accomplishments. When the nobleman found that the first servant had expanded his money a thousandfold, he didn't say, "Good! I get more money!" Rather, he said to the servant, "I'm impressed with *you*!" (Luke 19:17, paraphrase). The nobleman was interested in who that servant was as a person.

This is what God is always working for. His treasures are not the output of your work. *What God gets out of your life is the person you become.*[1]

5. Consider the statement that "what God gets out of your life is the person you become." What kind of person are you interested in becoming (or becoming more like) in the next six months? What kind of person would you like to become in the next year?

6. Take a few moments to ask God to show you an area in your life where you can *practice* faith in his kingdom (see how it works, move with it, and know that it's real). Write what you sense he is revealing in the space below. Now

acknowledge to God, "I see that you want me to do this. I know that you are here with me. I know that you will act with me."

Bringing Our Kingdom into God's Kingdom

Perhaps you're wondering exactly what your "kingdom" is. What you have say over may include any kind of educational pursuits, physical pursuits, talents, financial resources, or how you choose to treat people. You are in charge of your body, and you are here to use that body as the place of honoring God and blessing others. Seen in this light, even your work becomes not just your job but the total amount of good that you can accomplish over your lifetime in your relationship with your neighbors, your congregation, and the poor in your community.

Life becomes more fruitful and interesting as you learn to do your job, care for family members, buy a car, or do anything else while keeping this question in mind: *How would Jesus live my life if he were me?* Jesus had a job that likely involved managing the family carpentry business after Joseph died. As the oldest son, it also fell to him to manage the family. No doubt, Jesus bought tools and did other things like watching the games the children of Nazareth played. (Was he the referee?) These everyday things are part of our kingdom.

By the Holy Spirit's empowerment and your cooperation, you gradually do these things with the heart and character that Jesus would do them, handling the ordinary events of life in the way that he would. As you bring all these details into your life with God, you find you're able to love those around you, even those who annoy you or oppose you.

Nothing is too small for God to care about, because *faithfulness*—your loyalty, constancy, and devotion—makes a difference. Much of the good you accomplish is your investment in people, including children, grandchildren, and nieces and nephews, which often occurs in the way you are with them in small conversations. You can talk with God about how you want those relationships to develop, which will have incredible effects.

Perhaps you have a deep investment in your church and your fellowship with others there. Don't minimize simple things such as working with the sound equipment or providing coffee or teaching children. That is part of the creative good you produce in your kingdom.

Remember that your kingdom is not limited to just religious things. Dorcas made clothes and gave them to people who needed them (see Acts 9:36–43). Your kingdom may include anything from artwork to community volunteering, or from business organization to prayer ministries. All these things are places where you might say, "Yes, this is for me to do."

7. What are some everyday activities in your life, even small ones, that you could bring to God and talk about how Jesus would do them?

8. Much of our privilege and responsiblity in the kingdom is investing in people. Who are the people who have invested in you? Who are you investing in? (If you're not certain, take a few minutes to ponder what God may be inviting you into.)

Adjusting Our View of God

It is not uncommon for people to have the wrong view of God and not know him, even though they *think* they do. Some people, like the third servant in the parable, find God menacing and impossible to please. Perhaps this is because they haven't heard the gospel accurately, so they have never been exposed to the tenderness and gentleness that is in Jesus. Or perhaps they had the misfortune of an upbringing with unkind caregivers and now think of God in terms of those very bad examples. So they don't take responsibility and move forward with God.

When the basic motivation for our interactions with God is *fear*, we will hide from him and not open ourselves up to him. Fear drives us into a corner, making us lonely, frightened, and suspicious of people. Our fear can also make us think the way forward is to try and earn favor or bargain with God—sort of a quid pro quo game of *If I do X for God, God will do Y for me*. This leads to us feeling we deserve God's benefits because we did certain things for him, which, in turn, leads to frustration when God doesn't respond in the way that we want. All of this bypasses the lively conversation and rich life we can have with God if we work together.

Sometimes, we are frightened of God because we have the wrong idea about his greatness. God is great, but not in the same manner as humans. He is not like executives at huge corporations who have layers in place to separate him and his employees. God's greatness is seen precisely in his lowliness. Perhaps Jesus' smallest miracle was helping Peter pay a temple tax by finding a coin hidden in a fish's mouth (see Matthew 17:24–27). Imagine God helping you to pay your taxes! God is ready, willing, and able to deal with issues of any size. His care and love go out to all people, no matter how insignificant they might say they are.

Life with God is one that is full of courage, not fear. We identify our "minas" (health, mental development, relationships, work), take responsibility for them, and then invest in them for God's glory. Then, like the servant who made ten minas from one, we use those things to prepare for the fuller life that God has for us as we step into his purposes.

9. Perhaps you are surprised by the statement that "God's greatness is seen precisely in his lowliness." Consider these interactions that God had with people in the Bible:

- To get Jacob to interact and converse with him, God sent an angel disguised as an expert wrestler—of all things! (see Genesis 32:22–32).
- When the men in Elisha's school of prophets were upset because an ax-head they had borrowed tumbled into the water, Elisha cut off a stick and threw it in the water, which made the ax-head float (see 2 Kings 6:5–6).

- Jesus cooked breakfast for his disciples—and provided fish when those professional fishermen couldn't find fish! (see John 21:5–13).

How did God demonstrate his greatness in each of these acts of lowliness?

10. In the Bible, we read that "the fear of the LORD is the beginning of wisdom, and knowledge of the Holy One is understanding" (Proverbs 9:10). Inappropriate fear of God is different from the "fear of the Lord" described in this verse (and other places in Scripture). While inappropriate fear of God may cause you to hide from God, how might appropriate "fear of the Lord" help you take responsibility for all God has given you?[2]

Responding to What Jesus Said

Cultivating Your Life in the Kingdom of God Right Now

As you think about this, recognize the things over which you have some control. You might want to look at what you invest your energy and time in and say, "These are my 'minas.' My 'talents.' I'm going to invest them." We each have a purpose, and we are put here to count.

As you do this, you may decide that it's best *not* to be in charge of certain things. For example, it's certainly better not to be in charge of your neighbors and the way they behave. In a world saturated with busyness, we typically find that we are involved in too many distractions and are not deeply invested in the more crucial things of God.

Next, be definite about what you want to see happen. Many times in our prayers, we don't get anywhere because we haven't made a specific request. We pray, "Bless him!" and God answers, "Well, how? What do you want me to do to bless him?" Jesus instructed his disciples to specifically pray, "Give us today our daily bread" (Matthew 6:11). We need to understand the importance of being intentional and definite in our requests.

Finally, make sure your desired outcomes are of God. If you feel you are able to teach a class, or are developing investment banking, or are practicing law, let your expectation be *of God*. Try big things that you know you can't do by yourself—where the desired result is not within your power and you must rely on God's power to work. *Evidence of the presence of the Spirit of God is the incommensurability of the outcome with the effort.* This is where the outcome is so outstanding that it almost makes no sense compared to the small amount of effort put into it. When you see that tremendous difference in outcomes, you know that God is on the scene. This is what you really must do to cultivate the kingdom of God in your life.

11. Think about the statement, "Evidence of the presence of the Spirit of God is the incommensurability of the outcome with the effort." An example would be the scared disciples in the upper room who gathered together after Jesus' ascension. All they did was obey Jesus' instructions and pray, but the outcome was outstanding—they started a movement that spread as far (and even farther) than they could travel (see Acts 2). That's the work of the Holy Spirit. What does the possiblity of God doing something wonderful with your small efforts make you want to say to God right now?

12. Take on the challenge of praying specifially for those whom you typically offer a "bless him or her" type prayer. Begin by getting quiet and asking God to help you. See who comes to mind—maybe it's only one or two people. Then ask God how you might pray specifically for those individuals. Again, be quiet and see what comes to you. Whatever comes, write it down in the space below! Now look at it and see how it might form a prayer. Look at it again twenty-four hours later and see if anything else has come to you.

Key Terms

Kingdom or queendom: The things you have say over, where your decisions dictate what is done. This may include your actions (cleaning or yardwork), how you say things or talk to people, what you do with your leisure time, or what your motivation is behind your work.

Fear of the Lord: This term does not refer to being scared of the Lord or what he might do but rather holding him in reverence and awe. All followers of Jesus are commanded to do this: "Therefore, since we are receiving a kingdom that cannot be shaken, let us be thankful, and so *worship God acceptably with reverence and awe*" (Hebrews 12:28, emphasis added).

Talent: A common unit of money in Jesus' day. Estimates of its value vary for two primary reasons: (1) a talent could be of gold, silver, or copper, each with its own value; (2) a talent was first a measure of weight (between fifty-eight and eighty pounds) and then a unit of coinage, with a common value assigned to it of 6,000 denarii (see key terms in lesson 11). For this reason, it is often better to value the talent in terms of its earning power in the day. In that time, a typical servant earned about one denarius a day, so a talent represented approximately 6,000 days of a laborer's wages, or twenty years of labor (assuming a six-day workweek).[3]

Mina: Also a common unit of money in Jesus' day. The value of a mina was less than a talent—roughly one hundred denarii, or one-third of a laborer's yearly wages—so this represents a difference between Luke's and Matthew's versions of the parable (see Matthew 25:14–30). However, the principle that Jesus was making in each version remains the same.[4]

For Further Reading

Dallas Willard, *Renewing the Christian Mind: Essays, Interviews, and Talks* (San Francisco: HarperOne, 2016).

Jan Johnson, *Living a Purpose-Full Life: What Happens When You Say Yes to God* (Colorado Springs, CO: Waterbrook Press, 1999).

Kenneth Bailey, *Jesus Through Middle Eastern Eyes: Cultural Studies in the Gospels* (Lisle, IL: InterVarsity Press, 2008), chapter 31.

Christopher Wright, *The Mission of God's People: A Biblical Theology of the Church's Mission* (Grand Rapids, MI: Zondervan Academic, 2010), about how mission and theology, service and devotion go together.

Notes

1. Willard, *Renewing the Christian Mind*, 265.
2. The fear of the Lord is the beginning of wisdom; pure, enduring forever; hatred of evil; what prolongs life; life indeed; strong confidence. The reward for humility and fear of the Lord is riches and honor and life. See Psalm 111:10; Proverbs 9:10; Psalm 19:9; Proverbs 8:13; 10:27; 19:23; 14:26; 22:4.
3. D. A. Carson, *Matthew*, in *The Expositor's Bible Commentary*, vol. 9 (Grand Rapids, MI: Zondervan Academic, 2010), commentary on Matthew 25:15, 579–580.
4. Walter L. Liefeld and David W. Pao, *Luke*, in *The Expositor's Bible Commentary*, vol. 10 (Grand Rapids, MI: Zondervan Academic, 2007), commentary on Luke 19:12–14, 289.

LESSON 8

REVOLUTIONIZING LEADERSHIP: THE WELL-KEPT KINGDOM HEART

Parable of the Vineyard Owner and Corrupt Tenants (Luke 20:9–17)

Above all else, guard your heart, for everything you do flows from it.

PROVERBS 4:23

Understanding the contrast between the inner and outer person is absolutely fundamental. Christianity is a religion of the heart. This doesn't mean that external behavior is unchanged but rather that the root of Christian faith *and behavior* is found in the heart. No matter how much good behavior people display, they haven't got the real thing if they don't have a good heart. Doing God's will must come from the heart. (Recall from what we discussed in lesson 3 that the "heart" does not refer to feelings as it does in contemporary culture. The "will," the "spirit," and the "heart" are the same fundamental component of the person. See the key terms in that lesson.)

People can do good things with a wrong heart or a misguided heart. Jesus warned against following those who appear to be good but inwardly are governed by their own desires: "Not everyone who says to Me, 'Lord, Lord,' shall enter the kingdom of heaven, but he who does the will of My Father in heaven" (Matthew 7:21 NKJV). *Anyone* can call Jesus "Lord," but *following* Jesus as his apprentice in all of life is an entirely different thing.

Turning our hearts toward Christ and following his commands goes much deeper than just calling him "Lord." It requires us to have a special kind of life with Jesus where there is loving communication between us as we do the will of the Father. The will of the Father is to act and live as Jesus taught and become increasingly loving, humble, kind, forgiving, gracious—all the things that are also laid out in Paul's description of love in 1 Corinthians 13.

Jesus went on to explain this even further by painting a scene in which people announced how they had prophesied, driven out demons, and performed miracles, all in his name. He said, "Then I will tell them plainly, 'I never knew you. Away from me, you evildoers!'" (Matthew 7:23). These people didn't do God's will, even though they did miraculous works. This signals to us how relational God desires to be with us. He is not just a get-it-done-now or get-it-done-with-excellence kind of God but is also deeply interested in us and helping us become transformed into Christlikeness in our inward being.

Notice that Jesus didn't say, "*You* don't know me." He said, "*I* never knew you." This is both troubling and revealing. Have we allowed Jesus to *know* us? It's much like saying we *know* a famous person, but that person doesn't know us because we are not a part of his or her life. It matters whether we have an *interactive* life with God or only *know* about God.

Knowing and being known are important realities in our "with God" life. Knowledge is interactive relationship. George Eldon Ladd, a minister and professor of New Testament theology, said it well: "Knowledge in the Bible is far more than intellectual apprehension. Knowledge means experience. Knowledge means personal relationships. Knowledge means fellowship."[1]

1. "To have our hearts turned toward Christ" is a lovely phrase. But what do you think it actually means? What does it involve on your part?

2. What especially stands out to you when you consider having a *special kind of life with Christ* where there is *loving communication* between both of you? What would need to happen or change for you to have that kind of relationship with Jesus?

Hearing What Jesus Said

Jesus told the Parable of the Vineyard Owner and Corrupt Tenants shortly after he entered Jerusalem for the last time. He had just been questioned by the Jewish leaders about the source of his authority. As part of his response, he offered this parable to help them think.

> He went on to tell the people this parable: "A man planted a vineyard, rented it to some farmers and went away for a long time. At harvest time he sent a servant to the tenants so they would give him some of the fruit of the vineyard. But the tenants beat him and sent him away empty-handed" (Luke 20:9–10).

The vineyard owner did the work of planting the vineyard and then leased it to tenants to take care of the vines. The owner was not nearby, so the tenant-vinedressers apparently thought they could do whatever they wanted with the property and what it produced.

> "He sent another servant, but that one also they beat and treated shamefully and sent away empty-handed. He sent still a third, and they wounded him and threw him out.
>
> "Then the owner of the vineyard said, 'What shall I do? I will send my son, whom I love; perhaps they will respect him.'
>
> "But when the tenants saw him, they talked the matter over. 'This is the heir,' they said. 'Let's kill him, and the inheritance will be ours.' So they threw him out of the vineyard and killed him.
>
> "What then will the owner of the vineyard do to them? He will come and kill those tenants and give the vineyard to others" (Luke 20:11–16).

The Jewish people of that day would have recognized the vineyard as representing Israel, just as this image had represented Israel in Old Testament prophecies. The messengers were easy to recognize as the Old Testament prophets whom Israel had ignored. The parable thus portrayed how Israel had missed out on being faithful to God from the heart and also how they had missed out on their original calling to be a blessing to all nations, especially the marginalized (see Genesis 12:3; 28:14). The murder of the vineyard owner's son was, of course, a prophecy of what was about to happen in the final week of Jesus' life.

> When the people heard this, they said, "God forbid!"
>
> Jesus looked directly at them and asked, "Then what is the meaning of that which is written:
>
> " 'The stone the builders rejected
> has become the cornerstone'?
>
> "Everyone who falls on that stone will be broken to pieces; anyone on whom it falls will be crushed."
>
> The teachers of the law and the chief priests looked for a way to arrest him immediately, because they knew he had spoken this parable against them. But they were afraid of the people (Luke 20:16–19).

Jesus' reference to "that which is written" is from Psalm 118:22. He used this image of stonemasons separating the stones for sections of a proposed building to describe what was going to happen to him. Jesus stood for the keystone, about which the leaders were, in effect, saying, "That one will not do. Let's throw that one away. We cannot build our kingdom on Jesus Christ, his principles, and his way of life." Jesus was saying he was the most essential stone—the part that holds the building together. Just as Daniel predicted, he was the stone "cut out of a mountain, but not by human hands" (Daniel 2:45) that fills the entire earth.

3. What character qualities are evident in the vineyard owner? Why did he decide to send his own son to the tenants after they had beaten three of his servants?

4. How were the tenant workers presumptuous (not only arrogant but also illogical) in thinking they could do whatever they wanted with the vineyard?

Thinking About What Jesus Said

The Patience of God

The Parable of the Vineyard Owner and Corrupt Tenants describes God's often strained relationship with the people of Israel from Genesis 12 to Malachi 4 and beyond into the Gospels. It contradicts those who say that God was impatient with, tired of, or even vengeful toward Israel in Old Testament times. It shows the reality of God's patience throughout Israel's history as the people continually violated their covenant with God.

As recorded in Joshua to 2 Chronicles, the Israelites repeatedly turned their backs on God and allowed themselves to be influenced by the pagan ways of the people living with them in the promised land. They wanted kings instead of God as their leaders—and most of those kings didn't follow God. As a result, the Lord allowed the ten northern tribes (known as the kingdom of Israel) to be defeated and scattered, while the two southern tribes (known as the kingdom of Judah) lived in captivity for a few generations and then were restored.

However, in their restoration, the people became lax in their faithfulness. By Jesus' time, their faith was more about tithing from their spice racks and measuring their (lack of) miles traveled on the Sabbath. It was not a faith of loyalty and love toward God. It was about keeping rules and regulations, which could easily be shown off to others.

Throughout Israel's history, God was patient with his people and refused to give up on them. He gave them chance after chance, sending prophet after prophet, some of whom were persecuted and even killed: "They were put to death by stoning; they were sawed in two; they were killed by the sword" (Hebrews 11:37). When Jesus came, he still did not give up on the Jewish leaders, even meeting with one leader who was a seeker (see John 3).

Think about the vineyard owner in Jesus' parable. He planted the vineyard himself, creating new life and beauty. He gave the tenants jobs, which people truly need. In the same way today, God is patient, sending us person after person to show us his kindness. We see in them a better way to live, and in so doing, God woos us into goodness. When we err and make mistakes, he gives us chance after chance to change our ways. How God must weep when we ignore him and what he has done for us, pretending that he doesn't matter!

Like the vineyard workers, we have been given a beautiful place to live where we can sustain ourselves and have the possibility of creating some kind of good for others. We have a God of love and patience to thank for it.

5. Storytellers today seek to entertain or inspire, but Jesus told parables largely to disturb people and make them think. Jesus' portrayal of the vineyard owner is almost beyond comprehension. What do you think Jesus was trying to say by creating a character like this vineyard owner who sent representatives instead of a gang of skilled fighters?

6. Think about God's patience with you—in developing your character, in helping you see his love, in offering love to others. Write a sentence or two in response to this.

Authority Based on Ability

As previously noted, according to Luke, Jesus told the Parable of the Vineyard Owner and Corrupt Tenants during the first part of the final week of his life as he journeyed toward the cross. He had just entered Jerusalem, having been greeted with joy and palms by the common people (see Luke 19:28–38). However, the power structure of Israel was against him.

The religious leaders opposed him on a simple point: he threatened to undermine their authority by his own God-given authority, which they had not licensed. (Remember that just before Jesus told this parable, they had questioned him about the source of his authority.) While it was obvious that Jesus knew more about God, the Scriptures, and people than they did, they objected to his teaching because he had no human qualifications that they recognized.

Many organizations today, religious and otherwise, regard authority in the same way. They issue certificates to indicate that someone has the authority to act on behalf of the organization. Generally speaking, you can't fix a car, teach math, or preach in a church without the required certificate. But that certificate doesn't necessarily mean that you are actually *able* to do it. There is a different kind of authority that comes from ability. You may not be authorized to make the most delicious cheesecake in town or set up a computer system, but you still may be able to do it—and do it quite well. In such cases, other people rely on you and see you as an authority, even though you are not certified in any way.

The people of Israel had long suffered under leaders who had the backing (certification) of the Jewish leaders but didn't have the kind of authority that comes only from ability. Jesus didn't have the high priest's stamp of approval, so, in their eyes, he didn't deserve to be recognized as having authority. It's like saying to someone who is good at playing the piano, "Where did you get the authority to make such great music?" The person would probably laugh and say, "You don't need authority to make music. You just need to know *how to do it.*"

Authority comes from two sources: God and humans. Human authority can be obtained by passing tests to receive certification. But God looks much deeper into the heart when he is giving his authority to see if the person truly knows his reality in their inner life.

7. How does a person with a well-kept kingdom heart relate to ability—the acquiring of it, the desire for it, or the sharing of it?

8. It has been said there are four kinds of authority: (1) *positional* authority (you do what someone says because he or she is the boss), (2) *expert* authority (you do what someone says because he or she seems to understand things and explain them well), (3) *relational* authority (you do what someone says because of your deep attachment to him or her) and (4) *spiritual* authority (you do what someone says because you see in him or her the wisdom of God). Which of these types of authority do you find yourself the most influenced by? Explain your response.

Letting Go of Impression Management

The Pharisees were very concerned with their image. When Jesus criticized them for loving "greetings in the marketplaces" (Matthew 23:7 ESV), he was not referring to ordinary greetings.

When the Pharisees met certain people, they spoke with loud voices to "one up" them with all sorts of clever compliments and phraseology that would, at the same time, reflect glory on themselves. They sat in the highest seats in the synagogue where everyone would notice them. Dallas Willard called this tendency "impression management." It involves arranging our words, actions, and outward appearance to create the impression we want people to have of us.

Jesus didn't live in the bondage of trying to impress people. He could say difficult things to the crowds not just because he believed it would help them but also because he wasn't concerned with being honored and liked. He once said to those following him, "I do not accept glory from human beings" (John 5:41). This is often called living to "an audience of one" (God). As Richard Foster noted, this practice "is immensely simple: everything we do in life . . . we do before God alone and to the glory of God alone and with a view to pleasing God alone—the audience of One."[2] We walk through life with nothing to prove and no one to impress.

We can't truly trust God if we are trapped by our concerns of what other people think of us or if we are seeking to impress them with exaggerations and "tooting our own horn." We are trusting *ourselves* and *others* and putting ourselves in God's place. If we are truly concerned about the strength of our faith, we may need to seek God's grace in rooting out any desire to be honored by people. God's empowerment is needed because it is a struggle we all share.

On the other hand, we may struggle with hearing these words from God (and perhaps others): "Well done, good and faithful servant" (Matthew 25:23). This is especially true if we feel shame over things we have done in the past or don't feel as if we are "worthy" for God to say this about us. Yet we would do well to remember that "there is now no condemnation for those who are in Christ Jesus" (Romans 8:1) and that God sees us as his "special possession" (1 Peter 2:9). We can also do a great service to those who have selflessly made efforts to help others in some way by saying these words to them in a private moment. If they know we aren't prone to giving flattery, they may find our offering these words so helpful.

9. What are some situations in which you struggle the most with "impression management"? (For example, someone asks, "Have you read this book?" and without thinking, you say, "Yes, I've read it!") What else comes to mind?

10. How easy or difficult is it for you to hear these words from God: "Well done, good and faithful servant"? Who is someone in your life who needs to hear these words?

Responding to What Jesus Said

Cultivating an Inward Life

Christians can, without realizing it, base their decisions for doing something on this question: *What will people think if I do X?* Yet this concern for managing their image fades, and the character of Christ shows through, as they prioritize a connection with God that is vibrant, active, and determined. A well-kept kingdom heart overflows quietly and is observed over time.

Such a connection develops through ongoing practices that shape the inner dimensions of our lives. These disciplines for life in the Spirit enable us to do what we cannot do without such training—control our anger, our lusts, our speech, our reactions, and the like. Such spiritual disciplines are a means of drawing grace into our souls and bodies and transforming our habits (what we are ready to do without thinking) into godly character.

Here are a few practices that are especially helpful when it comes to impression management:

- **Solitude and silence:** The practice of being alone in quiet without speaking. This breaks the urge to be "in charge" and care about how others see us.
- **Secrecy in doing good:** Not telling everyone about all the good deeds that we have done but just rejoicing with the "audience of one."
- **Fasting:** Abstaining from food (or certain foods) or activities to affirm the Word of God and its sufficiency to our body. This is not merely skipping meals or other activities but intentionally devoting time to interacting with God.

- **Worship:** Focusing on God's goodness and relishing what he does: "The LORD is good to all; he has compassion on all he has made" (Psalm 145:9).
- **Learning Scripture by heart:** The practice of memorizing passages (such as 1 Corinthians 13, Colossians 3:1–17, or John 15) in such a way that they restructure our thoughts and feelings and spread to our whole lives.

The first three disciplines listed are those of *abstinence*, which are efficacious for learning to be sweet when we don't get what we want. The last two on the list are slow and steady disciplines of *engagement* that can permeate our lives.

11. Is there a passage of Scripture that you wish you knew so that you could have it in your mind when driving or standing in line at a store? If so, which one? (Write the reference out below.) If you are willing, study it and meditate on it for a month until it is familiar to you. Then ask God to show you the best method for committing it to memory.

12. If you were to have a time of solitude and silence each day, what might that look like? (Write it out below.) Know that it is okay to start small—ten minutes after lunch every day, or perhaps a morning spent hiking, or a quiet evening by a fireplace.

Key Terms

Knowledge: In biblical language and tradition, knowledge is never a mere acquisition of facts but is always an interactive relationship.[3] Once again, George Eldon

Ladd said it well: "Knowledge in the Bible is far more than intellectual apprehension. Knowledge means experience. Knowledge means personal relationships. Knowledge means fellowship."[4]

Living to an audience of one: Interacting with God about motives and receiving affirmation and guidance solely from him.

Eternal kind of life: Knowing the only true God and his Son, Jesus Christ, as an interactive, experiential relationship resulting in a daily life caught up in the life of God.

For Further Reading

Dallas Willard, "Spiritual Disciplines, Spiritual Formation and the Restoration of the Soul," chapter 8 in *The Great Omission: Reclaiming Jesus' Essential Teachings on Discipleship* (San Francisco: HarperOne, 2006).

Richard Foster, *Celebration of Discipline: The Path to Spiritual Growth* (San Francisco: HarperSanFrancisco, 1978).

Diana Shiflett, *Spiritual Practices in Community: Drawing Groups into the Heart of God* (Lisle, IL: InterVarsity Press, 2018).

John Bowen, *The Unfolding Gospel: How the Good News Makes Sense of Discipleship, Church Mission, and Everything Else* (Minneapolis, MN: Fortress Press, 2021), about the gospel and leadership.

Notes

1. George Eldon Ladd, *The Gospel of the Kingdom* (Grand Rapids, MI: Eerdmans, 1990), 71.
2. Richard Foster, "Growing Edges," *Perspectives*, vol. 4, no. 2 (April 1994), https://s3.amazonaws.com/renovareassets/downloads/newsletters/perspective_04_2.pdf.
3. Dallas Willard, *Knowing Christ Today* (New York: HarperCollins, 2009), 16, 151.
4. Ladd, *The Gospel of the Kingdom*, 71.

LESSON 9

LOST AND FOUND

Parable of the Prodigal Son (Luke 15:11–32)

This father so loved his son that forgiveness was his only course of action.

DALLAS WILLARD

To be *lost* means we are not where we are supposed to be. We may be aware we are lost, or we might be lost while sincerely believing we are in the right place. To be lost from God is to be disconnected from him. The giving, forgiving, reconciling heart of God yearns to find those who are lost. As he helps us find our way, his heart is full of mercy. It is never condemning.

When Jesus confronted Paul on the road to Damascus, he didn't condemn him or preach to him about how his theology was in error. He just spoke personally to him, asking, "Why do you persecute me?" (Acts 9:4), as if Paul were a friend who had betrayed him. Jesus gave him time to think (three years in Arabia) and people to guide him (Ananias and Barnabas). God showed tangible, relational mercy to someone who had murdered Christians en masse.

Paul did not see himself as lost. In fact, he believed he was doing a very good thing (see Acts 9:1–2). Many people today who are like Paul also don't see themselves as lost, perhaps because they come from a good family and have always succeeded. They never failed, felt out of place, or suffered the kinds of things that put them at the end of their rope.

Some of these "lost" folks recognize church as a good thing and join. They are intelligent people who feel they have it all together, so they pitch in and do good work, believing that God needs them to *help him*. In reality, they have a "church life" instead of a "life with God." They have a "working for God" life instead of a "living with God" life. They have not yet realized how much they need to be found by God.

Jesus warned his disciples about some of the people in their day who saw themselves as "God's helpers," saying, in effect, "There will come a day when they will give you up to death, and think they are doing God a favor" (see Matthew 24:9; Mark 13:11; Luke 21:12). Jesus wasn't saying such people were insincere. The people who crucified Jesus believed they were doing a good thing. To all these people, Jesus offered forgiveness (see Luke 23:34).

This lesson is on the Parable of the Prodigal Son, but if it were to be named after its hero, it might be called the Parable of the Loving Father, or the Parable of the Generous Father, or the Parable of the Merciful Father. The act of finding God, or the sense of being found by him, gives us a sense of being "washed over" with acceptance that we have never felt from anyone else. The God of the universe actually knows us and wants to be with us. He knows everything about us, even our worst moments, and still loves us. We finally belong somewhere.

1. What shift in thinking is necessary to move a person from having a "church life" to a "life with God"—and from a "for God" life to a "with God" life?

2. What does showing mercy and kindness look like to those who "have it all together," do good work, and believe that God needs them to help him?

Hearing What Jesus Said

The two brothers in the Parable of the Prodigal Son had different attitudes toward their father. The older son appeared to be concerned about pleasing his father and did everything that he could to help him. The younger son had assessed the situation at home and decided it was time to fend for himself. This is where our story begins:

> "A man had two sons. When the younger told his father, 'I want my share of your estate now, instead of waiting until you die,' his father agreed to divide his wealth between his sons. A few days later, the younger son packed all of his belongings and took a trip to a distant land" (Luke 15:11–13, paraphrase).

To be the younger son in those days was not a good position to have. When the father died, the oldest son inherited everything, and he then gave the other children whatever he wished to give them. So the younger son was not acting unreasonably when he asked for his inheritance while his father (whom he must have thought would be fair) was still alive. He seemed to have guessed that his older brother was not a giving, forgiving, or merciful person.

The father was no doubt troubled as his son walked out the door. Perhaps he prayed, "God, help him, and God, help me." Everything this father probably feared came true.

"And there he wasted all of his money on parties and prostitutes. And about the time his money was gone, a famine swept over the land and he began to starve. He persuaded a local farmer to allow him to feed his pigs. But the boy became so hungry that even the husks he was feeding the swine looked good to him. And no one gave anything to him" (Luke 15:13–16, paraphrase).

The younger son had many friends when he had money—but not so many when he was down and out. Caring for pigs was about as low as it could get for a Jewish man. Even worse, he was prepared *to eat what the pigs ate*. That seemed to wake him up.

"When he finally came to his senses, he said to himself, 'My father's servants eat better than this, while I'm going hungry. I'm going to go back and ask Dad for a job. I'll say, "You don't have to hire me, of course. But I need a job, and you treat your workers well." ' And while he was still a long distance away, his father saw him coming and was filled with loving pity, and ran to meet him, and fell on his neck, and kissed him" (Luke 15:17–20, paraphrase).

Imagine how the father felt during the time he waited to hear from his son. He may have sent a servant to check on him and knew that he worked in a pigpen. The father came *running* when he saw his son a long way off because he had been looking for him. He didn't close himself off, self-righteously judging his son. He hoped his son would return. Nor did the father insist that his son get cleaned up from the pigpen. Instead, he embraced him. The bath would come later. The father had probably forgiven him already.

"His son began to say to him, 'Father, I've sinned against heaven and against you, and I'm not worthy of being called your son.' But his father interrupted his story and said to the servants, 'Quick, bring the finest robe in the house and put it on him! And a jeweled ring for his finger, and shoes for his feet. And kill the calf we've been fattening. We must celebrate with a feast. For this son of mine was dead and has returned to life. He was lost, and now he is found.' And so the party began" (Luke 15:21–24, paraphrase).

3. What do you think it would feel like to be as lost as the younger son was in this story that Jesus told? What creates such a turnaround of heart?

4. It was one thing for the father to forgive his son, but quite another thing for the father to throw a party. What does this tell you about God (as portrayed by the father)?

Thinking About What Jesus Said

The Father's Heart Is Giving

In the Parable of the Prodigal Son, when the younger son requested his inheritance, the father could have easily refused. He could have said, "I know what you're going to do with it! I'm not giving it to you, because you are unreliable! You are so easily swayed." However, the father understood the difficulty his son was facing, and so he helped his son. He gave the younger son what he requested because the heart of the father is one that gives.

No doubt the father had grounds to worry about his son, but most children eventually mature to the point that parents take on the role of helping them do what they want to do. While this might seem dangerous, the children are won over by their giving, helping parents who have confidence in them. So we take the mercy we have received from God and show our children mercy. We say, "You want to dye your hair green or purple? Sit down. I'll help you."

Parents are meant to love their children, not squash them. And while parents often feel responsible for their children's behavior, there comes a moment when they have to turn them loose. Some children need to differentiate from their parents, so they go through another "terrible twos" stage when they reach adolescence or early adulthood. In essence, they say, "I'm not you, Mom. I'm not you, Dad." They don't know *who* they really are. But even in the heartbreak, the parents can remain confident because their confidence is in God.

As for the younger son in the parable, many people have found themselves in his place. Their choices have reduced them to doing things they never thought they would do, and they find themselves in the "pigpen." If they are rebelling against what they know is best, they feel as if they have to justify themselves. No doubt the younger son at some point justified himself, perhaps sitting on the fence of the pigpen and singing about what a great life he had.

Consider that it was the generosity of the father to his younger son that turned that son's heart toward home. The son seemed to understand his father's kindness and knew that his father would be kind to him. The kindness of God is what leads to repentance (see Romans 2:4). Yes, God is kind even to people who actually *prefer* to sin (see Luke 6:35).

5. In our culture of giving people in trouble "what they deserve," how does the idea that "the kindness of God leads people to repentance" really work in personal relationships?

6. How does a giving heart develop? What helps us move toward that place?

The Father's Heart Is Forgiving

In times past, and still today, some people have thought that forgiveness should be hard to obtain—that others need to work hard to earn it. This has led to people grinding away at each other, holding the other person's offense over their heads. But consider that when someone in our family—a spouse, child, or relative—has done something foolish, it isn't our job to make sure they know how wrong they've been. The forgiving heart yearns for the lost to come back.

The prophet Hosea illustrated this through the example of his own life. Hosea was a righteous man, a prophet and a teacher in Israel, somewhat like a pastor today. In order to present a message to the nation of Israel, God told Hosea to marry Gomer, a woman prone to unfaithfulness. Hosea's obedience meant that he had to endure the whispers, scandal, and questions as to whether the children running around his house were his own.

When Gomer was sold into slavery, the Lord came to him and said, "Go to the auction block where she's being sold and buy her back." Hosea did this, brought her home, and loved her once again (see Hosea 3:1–3). It was out of this story of Hosea's broken heart that Jesus—as he tried to help people understand the merciful, forgiving heart of God—said these words: "Go and learn what this means: 'I desire mercy, not sacrifice'" (Matthew 9:13; see Hosea 6:6).

Such a forgiving heart may take some time to acquire. When people ask to be forgiven, the one being asked may respond, "Of course." But the next day, they feel differently. In reality, they felt cornered into saying the right thing, when what they actually needed was time to work out the situation with God and perhaps receive healing and counsel. Forgiveness is a process, so mercy flows both ways: toward the one who committed the offense *and* toward the one attempting to forgive the offense. When that occurs, and forgiveness is then offered, it is genuine and long-lasting. The person doing the forgiving experiences the hand of God working in them and God's love flowing out of them. What a great experience!

7. Ask God to help you remember when someone has gone that extra mile to forgive you. What did you think at that moment? How did that feel?

8. If someone asks you point-blank for forgiveness, what would be the wisest thing to say if you are surprised and still need some time to process everything that happened?

The Father's Heart Is Reconciling

A great deal can be said for the older son in the Parable of the Prodigal Son. He may have watched with tears as his brother left. He may have done the younger brother's work while he was gone. But somehow, he never knew the depths of his father's love.

We see this in the way he acted when he returned from the fields and heard the music and dancing coming from the house. When he disocovered that his brother was back and the father had prepared a feast for him, he became angry and wouldn't go inside. His heart was quite unlike his father's heart, and he couldn't enter into that joy (see Luke 15:25–28).

Just as the father had gone out to meet the younger brother, he went out to the older brother. We can picture him sulking on the porch as his father *begged* him to have mercy on his brother. But instead of forgiving, the older son spoke with self-righteousness and self-pity: "All these years I've been slaving for you and never disobeyed your orders. . . . But when this son of yours who has squandered your property with prostitutes comes home, you kill the fattened calf for him!" (Luke 15:29–30). He was jealous of the love his father gave to his brother.

The father's heart was to *reconcile* the family. The father did not say to the older brother, "You're in trouble with me because your heart isn't right." Instead he said, "You are always with me, and everything I have is yours" (Luke 15:31). He not only forgave but also went to the one who thought he didn't *need* forgiveness and begged him to show mercy.

This parable is as much about the older brother as the younger one. Jesus addressed it to the grumbling Pharisees and scribes, who preferred to make sacrifices rather than live with a merciful heart. Jesus said those who show mercy are blessed (see Matthew 5:7), but evidently the Pharisees and scribes, just like the older son in the story, didn't believe it. They didn't see that being merciful, like the father in the story, was an act of one who is "blessed."

Many people today likewise insist on standing on their rights and believe that extending mercy to those who need it is wrong. It undermines their sense of security because the human systems we live in work by forcing and condemning people rather than simply showing mercy to them. But the father knew the power of mercy.

9. Where do you see yourself in this parable: the rebellious younger brother, the repentant younger brother, the bitter older brother, or the merciful father? Explain your response.

10. Many of us are on a journey of experiencing the truth that the older brother never knew: the depths of the father's love. What activities or simple practices help you to be immersed in God's love for you? (If you're not sure, simply ask God for ideas.)

Responding to What Jesus Said

The Power of Mercy

The surest way to lead someone in the path of goodness is to be merciful to them. The surest way to drive them into wrongdoing and anger is to be *un*merciful. It is the power of mercy that conquers the hardened heart. You may think, *It's okay* *for God to be merciful, but what's going to happen if I'm merciful? Won't they just do it again?* But it's only when you step into the path of mercy that you begin to live in the power of God. When you refuse to hold anything against another person, you experience the abundance of God to meet all your needs.

When a loved one goes astray, one of the typical problems is that one family member wants to be merciful while the others refuse. They are worried that mercy will be perceived as condoning the wrong behavior. Or perhaps they think they can control the offender by being unmerciful to them. Jesus taught against such condemnation engineering, saying, "Do not judge, or you too will be judged" (Matthew 7:1). He was dealing with people who believed they could control other people by condemning them—that the offender would stop doing evil things if they were condemned. Even today, people are convinced it's important to keep the condemnation coming, which bounces back as the other person condemns them in return.

When we look at the Parable of the Prodgal Son, we find that it is actually about the kingdom of God, even though that is not specifically mentioned. The connection is twofold. First, the father enacts the kingdom life in his merciful, reconciling heart. Second, as we live such a life, we experience the power of God's kingdom in our lives. We can show the father's kingdom heart to others, even those who disappoint us. The abundance of life, grace, and mercy we find in the kingdom of God can be extended to anyone and everyone.

11. God says to you the same words the father said to the older brother: "You are always with me, and everything I have is yours." How do you respond to this truth?

12. Which dimension of the father's heart do you need today: (1) *giving* you what you need, (2) *forgiving* your offenses, or (3) *reconciling* you to yourself and others? Which of these do you find the most challenging to extend to others? Explain your response.

Key Term

Forgiveness: Letting someone "off the hook" and no longer blaming that person who has wronged or offended you.

For Further Reading

Henri Nouwen, *The Return of the Prodigal Son: A Story of Homecoming* (New York: Image Books, 1994).

Everett L. Worthington Jr., *Forgiving and Reconciling: Bridges to Wholeness and Hope* (Lisle, IL: InterVarsity Press, 2003).

Klyne Snodgrass, *Stories with Intent: A Comprehensive Guide to the Parables of Jesus* (Grand Rapids, MI: Wm. B. Eerdmans, 2018), chapter 6 on the Parable of the Prodigal Son.

LESSON 10

PREPARE THE WAY: ALERT FOR KINGDOM OPPORTUNITIES

Parables of the Ten Women and the Faithful and Unfaithful Servant (Matthew 25:1–13; Luke 12:42–48)

Our actions demonstrate the degree to which Jesus is our treasure.

DALLAS WILLARD

Many years ago, a wealthy man was looking for a driver for his coach. He tested the candidates by taking them to a section of road that ran alongside a cliff and instructed them to see how close they could drive to the edge. Most of the applicants were taken in by the challenge to prove their expertise and drove close to the edge without faltering. But one driver refused to drive close to the edge at all. He got the job because he had enough concern about the well-being of his passenger that he would never use the situation to show off his driving skills.

It is interesting to think of how each of the applicants might have described their driving skills if they had only been given an interview. Perhaps they all would have declared their driving to be highly skilled, quick, and efficient but still very safe. Only by riding with each one could the owner of the coach know how the driver would *actually* conduct himself. In the same way, who we really are is revealed by how we behave in unexpected situations.

People often defend their bad behavior by saying, "I was caught off guard," as if they normally guard everything they do in order to give the right impression. When we get into these kinds of situations where we surprise ourselves, it is wise for us to reflect on what was going on inside. What motives or leftover hurts were affecting us? We might recognize, "I didn't know I felt that way" or, "I didn't know I thought those things." Dallas Willard liked to point out how Jesus said in his final talk with his disciples, "I will no longer talk much with you, for the ruler of this world is coming, and he has nothing in Me" (John 14:30 NKJV). Satan had nothing "in" Jesus—no hidden hurts, resentments, or desires that would lead him to sin.

The Parable of the Talents (which we discussed in lesson 7), the Parable of the Ten Women, and the Parable of the Faithful and Unfaithful Servant (which we will explore in this lesson) each show how people's actions reveal what is in their hearts, which then reveals the degree to which they treasure Jesus. In the Parable of the Talents, it came to light that the servant with one mina (or talent) didn't know his master at all, saying to him, "I knew you were hard" (Matthew 25:24, paraphrase). In his master's absence, he calculated how little he could do, how much he could get away with, and still please his master. The servant was obviously aware of what was in his heart, and so he was willing to cut it close.

In the Parable of the Ten Women, we will likewise discover what was in the hearts of five of the women who were considered "foolish" because they did as little as possible (not taking oil for their lamps) as they waited for the bridegroom to arrive. In the Parable of the Faithful and Unfaithful Servant, we will explore what was in the heart of the "unfaithful" servant who also slacked on his responsibilities—to the point of abusing other servants—while he waited for his master to return. Allow these parables to help reveal if you are willing to do as little as possible to please God or if you want your whole heart to seek after him.

1. In the illustration of the coach drivers, what did their behavior say about their view of the owner? Or their potential future passengers?

2. Think of the last time your behavior surprised you—either good or bad. What do you now recognize was going on in your heart at that moment. (If you are not sure, ask God to help you see if there's something about yourself that you need to know.)

Hearing What Jesus Said

Like many of Jesus' other stories, the Parable of the Ten Women features a rich person (in this case a bridegroom) who goes away and is a "long time" in returning home. This was a common occurrence with which Jesus' listeners would have been familiar.

> "Then the kingdom of heaven will be like this. Ten young women took their lamps and went to meet the bridegroom. . . . As the bridegroom was delayed, all of them became drowsy and slept" (Matthew 25:1, 5 NRSVUE).

Imagine an estate with a large house and several barns. These women appear to have been household aids or perhaps village girls who had come to help with the wedding. Their job was to wait in the lane with their lamps burning to light the path for the bridegroom and the bride when they came back. But the wedding party was delayed. Of the ten women, five saw the possibility of a delay (wedding parties celebrated by taking the longest way home!) and wisely brought extra oil in a flask to refill their lamps when they ran out. The other five did not. Maybe they thought, *I have enough oil in the lamp. It will be okay.*

> "But at midnight there was a shout, 'Look! Here is the bridegroom! Come out to meet him'" (Matthew 25:6 NRSVUE).

When the servant stationed down the road shouted that the bridal party was approaching, the women shook themselves awake. They prepared their lamps, which was when one of the five unwise women said, "Uh-oh!"

> "The foolish said to the wise, 'Give us some of your oil, for our lamps are going out.' But the wise replied, 'No! there will not be enough for you and for us; you had better go to the dealers and buy some for yourselves'" (Matthew 25:8–9 NRSVUE).

We shouldn't assume the five wise women were stingy or mean. They were just being sensible. If they gave some of their oil to the others, they would run out more quickly, and then there wouldn't be enough oil to provide light for the bridegroom and bride. Their suggestion for the other women to buy the oil was a good idea. Everyone knew everyone in such villages, so acquiring a little oil from someone was not a problem, even in the middle of the night.

> "And while they went to buy it, the bridegroom came, and those who were ready went with him into the wedding banquet, and the door was shut" (Matthew 25:10 NRSVUE).

"Those who were ready" formed the wedding party and went to the wedding. The organizers didn't want people entering in the middle of the ceremony, so they shut the door.

> "Later the other young women came also, saying, 'Lord, lord, open to us.' But he replied, 'Truly I tell you, I do not know you'" (Matthew 25:11–12 NRSVUE).

The wise women were prepared to serve the bridegroom well. He *knew* them. But the other five did not make preparations, and so the bridegroom did *not know* them.

3. What did the actions of the five unwise women reveal about their normal disposition as it relates to their role in the household?

4. What was the significance of the bridegroom not knowing the five unwise women? (Note that Jesus had referred to himself as the bridegroom before in Matthew 9:15.)

Thinking About What Jesus Said

Conscious of God's Blessing

The Parable of the Ten Women is often paired with the Parable of the Faithful and Unfaithful Servant found in Luke 12:42–48. In this story, Jesus tells of a faithful manager who gave his servants their portion of food at the right time. Jesus said of him, "Blessed is that servant whom his master will find so doing when he comes. Truly, I say to you that he will make him ruler over all that he has" (Luke 12:43–44 NKJV). Those whose hearts are focused on God constantly have him and his kingdom agenda on their minds, and it is never a burden. They are blessed!

But there is another servant in the story—an unfaithful one. When he realized the master was delayed, he started to mistreat and even beat his fellow servants. This unfaithful servant didn't have the best interests of his master or the household in mind; instead, he calculated how much he could get away with doing. He didn't think that because he was now in charge, he should do a good job and take good care of things. His calloused ways revealed his disloyal, self-absorbed character and that he only treasured himself.

There are some people who do good things and appear to be good, but when the opportunity arises, they do whatever it takes to get what they want—even if they have to sin. Character is not about what people do but about what they would do or could do given the opportunity. This reveals where their heart has been aimed all along.

The same is true in our life with God. As we reflect on how much God has done for us and how much he treasures us, we become devoted to him. We want to partner with God in doing the good that he wants done on this earth. Jesus explained, "From everyone to whom much has been given, much will be required, and from the one to whom much has been entrusted, even more will be demanded" (Luke 12:48 NRSVUE). The phrase "much will be required" does not indicate the giving is forced. We have been given much and appreciate God's trust in us, and so it becomes natural for us to give deeply to others.

This should remind us of the illustration in lesson 3 about those with large buckets (receptivity to hear) that God fills with wisdom and goodness. It just makes sense that those buckets overflow with blessing for others.

5. What are some ways that people become "calculating" regarding family members, coworkers, or even friends? What do you think causes people to become this way?

6. Who are some of those people that you are so grateful for having in your life that you gladly, willingly, and even eagerly do your best to help them?

Alert Readiness to Move

At the conclusion of the Parable of the Ten Women, Jesus said to his listeners, "Therefore keep watch" (Matthew 25:13). The theme of *watching* in the New Testament often means alert readiness. It occurs often in the Old Testament with the term *watchman* (see Job 27:18; Psalm 127:1 NKJV; Isaiah 21:5–6 NKJV, 11–12; Ezekiel 3:17; 33:1–7; Hosea 9:8; Micah 7:4). Watchmen, who were lookouts or sentinels, were familiar figures in those days. They observed diligently and called out when attention and action were required.

Being *watchful* in our life with God is about walking alongside Jesus with intentionality and follow-through. It is about knowing and loving Jesus "for the long haul." Discipleship is not instantaneous. Maturation grows with our increasing awareness of God. We continually seek to know God personally, not ride on the coattails of others. This is an authentic journey with God, not a few moments of thinking that getting to know Jesus personally seems like a good idea and something that we should do.

Watchfulness is particularly important in times of stress. We see this illustrated in the story of Peter, James, and John in the garden of Gethsemane. In Jesus' sorrow and distress, he said to them, "My soul is exceedingly sorrowful, even to death. Stay here and watch with Me" (Matthew 26:38 NKJV). Shortly thereafter, he found them asleep. He said to Peter, "Could you not watch with Me one hour? Watch and pray, lest you enter into temptation. The spirit indeed is willing, but the flesh is weak" (Matthew 26:40–41 NKJV).

If someone had asked these disciples in the garden, "Are you willing to watch with Jesus?" they probably would have said yes. But they knew the officials were looking for Jesus and for them as well. They had not yet trained their bodies to follow Jesus even when they were afraid or unsure. So Jesus advised his friends to be watchful in an attitude of prayer. Staying alert would have provided them with a level of responsiveness and power that would otherwise have been impossible for them to achieve. As it turned out, they were *not* able to stand with Christ when his enemies confronted him, because they had not been watchful in prayer.

To truly be ready to move requires a devotion to Jesus—an experiential knowledge of him that tells us all will be well if we venture out. But it also requires for us to be diligent observers of ourselves, noticing when more intensity is needed in our motives and action.

7. What does it mean for you to "keep watch" when it comes to your life in Christ? What helps you to maintain "alert readiness" during times of stress and even anxiety?

8. Think of someone you know who has been with Jesus "over the long haul." Try to guess what has helped that person maintain "alert readiness." Write that in the space below. Then (really—do this!) call or meet with that person and ask what has helped him or her to do this. (You can explain it as having an "assignment" from this workbook.)

Watching for Opportunities

In the Parable of the Ten Women, all of the women were waiting for the bridegroom's return. Given that Jesus often referred to himself as the bridegroom (see, for example, Mark 2:19–20), it makes sense that many interpret the parable about the second coming of Christ. However, the parable is about more than just Jesus' return to this world. It is about spiritual opportunity in all of life, our readiness to seize the day, because the present moment—this day—is the only place where we live.

We cannot live in the past nor the future, so we don't dwell there. *Today* is the day of salvation (see 2 Corinthians 6:2). Salvation is, biblically speaking, deliverance. It provides us with forgiveness of sins but also ushers in a new order of life in which we are "delivered . . . from the power of darkness" (Colossians 1:13 KJV) and brought into the kingdom of the Son. In that kingdom—where what God wants done gets done—we have a different order of life. We are to live in and from a different world where it makes sense to trust God no matter what.

To *watch* means we encounter people in anticipation that this may be a moment to do or say whatever Jesus would do or say. And so, we watch for Jesus throughout the day. He may come to us in the form of a neighbor, a little child, a pastor, a teacher, a friend, or even an enemy. We see this in Jesus' metaphor of the sheep and goats, when the righteous asked:

> " 'Lord, when did we see you hungry and feed you, or thirsty and give you something to drink? When did we see you a stranger and invite you in, or needing clothes and clothe you? When did we see you sick or in prison and go to visit you?' The King will reply, 'Truly I tell you, whatever you did for one of the least of these brothers and sisters of mine, you did for me' " (Matthew 25:37–40).

This is not as hard as you might think. The five wise young women in the parable knew what they were about. They lived and did their job with intentionality and focus. Likewise, the faithful servant served in his role with intentionality and focus. They all prepared—just as we have—hearts that are made ready and refreshed by God.

9. Reflect on the last twenty-four hours. When, where, and through whom may Jesus have come to you? (Ask God to help you notice him more fully.)

10. If you weren't afraid, cautious, or just plain hesitant, how might you serve in a way that God seems to have in mind for you? (Relax. We're in the dreaming stage here.) What preparation would you make in prayer or in conversations with others?

Responding to What Jesus Said

Conversational Life with God

"Keeping watch" flows out of having lively back-and-forth conversations with God. This doesn't mean talking *at* God but rather asking him questions and then *listening* in the moments after you ask. Let's say, for example, your computer doesn't work. So you ask God for a next step. You're quiet and careful, and then the name of an old friend who knows computers comes to mind. Or you remember where the user guide is.

Computers, people's complaints, back surgery . . . all these things can seem insurmountable when we stand alone before them. But we have to remember that God is also here—really here! The kingdom of God is *here*. None of these things have to be faced all at once but can be faced in conversation after conversation with God. We ask, "What's next?" Then a next step comes to us. Relief! Then another conversation, and next step, and so on.

King David knew to do this—even in times of stress when the Philistine army was hovering around him. One time when he asked God if he should engage them, the Lord said, "Do not go directly after them, but circle around them and attack them in front of the poplar trees. As soon as you hear the sound of marching in the tops of the poplar trees, move out to battle, because that will mean God has gone out in front of you to strike the Philistine army" (1 Chronicles 14:14–16). As a result, the Israelites had an experience they certainly never forgot: they heard the audible sound of God moving in the trees! They knew God was with them.

The Israelites knew not to take one step until God did. They had the experience of moving only when God moved, of partnering with him in a fearful situation. David facilitated this because his heart was for the Lord. He watched, didn't opt out of conversation with God, and lived in the companionship and guidance of God. He moved when God moved.

11. Read 1 Chronicles 14:8–17 aloud slowly. Close your eyes and picture the scene and hear the sound of the marching. Sit in that. Then think of a situation about which you are bewildered or afraid or overwhelmed. Write that below, and ask God to help you.

12. What is something about which you would like to engage in conversation with God? What are some questions that you want to ask him right now about it?

Key Term

Watching: Walking alongside Jesus with intentionality and follow-through, encountering people in anticipation that this may be a moment to do or say whatever Jesus would do or say, and actively looking for such encounters.

For Further Reading

Bob Buford, "Is There Something More?," chapter 2 in *Finishing Well: The Adventure of Life Beyond Halftime* (Grand Rapids, MI: Zondervan, 2004).

David Wenham, *The Parables of Jesus* (Lisle, IL: InterVarsity Press, 1989), about the Parable of the Ten Women.

LESSON 11

THE MIRACLE OF FORGIVENESS

Parable of the Unforgiving Servant (Matthew 18:21–35)

Forgiveness can become a simple, straightforward act done because it is the best thing to do. . . . It's simply the wise thing to do.

DALLAS WILLARD

Forgiveness is a miracle. It's a tremendous act of grace that introduces people into the upside-down world of God. *Un*forgiveness is the way of normal, ordinary life. It is so embedded into society's way of thinking that many people do not even consider themselves to be unforgiving when they hold on to past wounds. They accept it as the status quo and just say, "Oh, that's just the way it is." It's also normal for certain nations to be enemies of each other.

The plots of countless novels and movies focus on "getting even." When children fight, that last punch or insult is what matters. Whatever was done last is somehow bigger than anything that came before it. International negotiations and courts often fail because they focus on trying to make people and nations "even." But getting even doesn't work.

It's the same in relationships between brothers and sisters and even between spouses. There is no peace as long as two parties are trying to get even. If one spouse offends the other, that person is deeply hurt. For a while, the one hurt may be peaceable, but the offense sits there in the heart and eats away at it. Before long, getting even looks like a good idea. So that person tries the silent treatment. But then both suffer. Getting even hurts everyone.

Furthermore, no one ever really gets even because what one person counts as "even" looks to the other person as being "behind." There cannot be a union of souls such as God intended until people rise above this. If unforgiveness ceased to be a part of human life, human history would be transformed beyond recognition and there would be peace.

The gospel of the Lord Jesus Christ means an end to this absurdity. It declares from the heights of heaven that *God doesn't want to even the score*. God invites us into a life where we no longer need to do that. This is an expression of the nature of the gospel of Jesus. This is the *only* way that peace can come to the human heart—and then the world. People who are forgiving lay down all plans to get even for wrongs done, even in small ways. They also let go of requiring compensation, no longer saying, "You must make it up to me!" Getting even is such a burden, and it's a great relief to let it go.

The way of life in the kingdom of God is to routinely and easily forgive, as illustrated by the king in the Parable of the Unforgiving Servant that we will explore in this lesson. We need this illustration because we just can't imagine how God forgives; it is impossible for us to conceive of it. So here, in this parable, we see the generosity of God's forgiveness toward us.

1. How have you seen it to be true that getting even is a burden? Why does getting even ultimately not make either of the parties involved feel good?

2. Which of the following phrases is the most difficult for you to believe: (1) forgiveness is a miracle, (2) no one ever really gets even, (3) the only way peace can come to the human heart is through forgiveness, or (4) the way of life in the kingdom of God is to routinely and easily forgive? Why is that phrase the most difficult for you to believe?

Hearing What Jesus Said

Jesus told the Parable of the Unforgiving Servant after Peter quizzed him about how many times he had to forgive someone who sinned against him. Peter had suggested "up to seven times." He was probably thinking, *I'll impress Jesus—seven times is a lot!* Of course, Jesus gave that now-famous answer: "Seventy times seven" (Matthew 18:21–22 NKJV). Perhaps Peter gulped at that. He thought he was already being more than generous. We can imagine Jesus smiling at Peter's reaction. Jesus was getting at the *legalistic way* of defining righteousness and forgiveness, and saying, "Counting times won't work. You have to cultivate a forgiving heart."

> "Therefore the kingdom of heaven is like a certain king who wanted to settle accounts with his servants. And when he had begun to settle accounts, one was brought to him who owed him ten thousand talents. But as he was not able to pay, his master commanded that he be sold, with his wife and children and all that he had, and that payment be made" (Matthew 18:23–25 NKJV).

Selling people into slavery to pay their debts was not uncommon at that time. Even a lodger in an inn who could not pay his bill risked being sold as a slave by the innkeepers.

> "The servant therefore fell down before him, saying, 'Master, have patience with me, and I will pay you all.' Then the master . . . was moved with compassion, released him, and forgave him the debt" (Matthew 18:26–27 NKJV).

Here was a king who no longer held accountable someone who had spent what amounts to 60,000,000 times one day's wage (one denarius) of his money.[1] The generous king did not postpone the debt or suggest payments but completely released the servant from the debt and forgave him. This *astounding* generosity no doubt stunned Jesus' listeners.

> "But that servant went out and found one of his fellow servants who owed him a hundred denarii; and he laid hands on him and took him by the throat, saying, 'Pay me what you owe!' So his fellow servant fell down at his feet and begged him, saying, 'Have patience with me, and I will pay you all'" (Matthew 18:28–29 NKJV).

Note the unbelievable contrast in the size of the debts (which was part of Jesus' teaching technique). The servant's fellow slave owed him a fraction of what he had just been forgiven. Both servants used the same language when their debts were called to account: "Have patience with me, and I will pay you all."

> "And he would not, but went and threw him into prison till he should pay the debt. So when his fellow servants saw what had been done, they were very grieved, and came and told their master all that had been done. Then his master, after he had called him, said to him, 'You wicked servant! I forgave you all that debt because you begged me. Should you not also have had compassion on your fellow servant, just as I had pity on you?' And his master was angry, and delivered him to the torturers until he should pay all that was due to him. So My heavenly Father also will do to you if each of you, from his heart, does not forgive his brother his trespasses" (Matthew 18:30–35 NKJV).

You can imagine Jesus' listeners aghast, with their mouths open and foreheads creased. So much was owed; so much was forgiven. But this forgiveness was not passed on.

3. Jesus' parables often included a character (or characters) who did rather unexpected and even outlandish things (which made them memorable). In what way was that true of the king? In what way was that true of the first servant who had been forgiven a great debt?

4. Read Matthew 18:30–35 again slowly. Pause. With which character do you most identify: the king, the first servant, or the second servant? What feelings do you have as this character? (When you're ready, talk with God about what has come to you.)

Thinking About What Jesus Said

Receiving the Gift of Forgiveness

It is impossible for us to forgive until we have experienced forgiveness ourselves. It's like love: "We love because he first loved us" (1 John 4:19). This is also the intent of the phrase "and forgive us our debts, as we forgive our debtors" in the Lord's Prayer (Matthew 6:12 NKJV; see also Matthew 6:14–15). However, people have unfortunately misunderstood this to mean that forgiveness from God is something to be earned by forgiving those who have offended us. Instead, *because* God has forgiven us, we are *equipped* to forgive our debtors.

God's forgiveness is not a matter of our earning it but our receiving it. It's important to distinguish between *earning* and *receiving.* While we cannot earn our salvation, we need to consciously receive it, and we're so much better off for doing so. Receiving it is not automatic, because a gift is not imposed on us. We can choose to take it or not take it. An imposition is something that is forced on us somehow, but a gift requires a reception.

The Parable of the Unforgiving Servant shows that in order for us to receive the forgiveness that comes from God, we must have a certain kind of heart and life shaped by the grace of God in us. When we concentrate on the work of Christ (his coming for us, his life, and his way of living) and become his apprentice, we step into the flow of that grace and can receive a forgiving heart. Such a heart can reach out in faith and accept forgiveness from God.

We saw some examples in lesson 9 of people who had no knowledge or understanding of a forgiving heart: the older brother in the Parable of the Prodigal Son, and the Pharisees who prompted the parable (see Luke 15:1–2). They didn't believe they had ever been lost, so they didn't believe that they needed saving. They did not have an *experience* of forgiveness.

Forgiveness is available because of the great heart of God revealed throughout history—a history that peaked on the cross when Jesus died. God made provision for our salvation in a way that invites us into his kind of life. Whatever God needed to be done to open the floodgates of his compassion on the world was done. Now it is our turn to experience this gift throughout the ups and downs of our lives.

5. Think of the first time the disciples saw Jesus after his resurrection. Perhaps they were afraid. They had fled and abandoned him. None of them had stood up for him, much less stood next to him. Yet Jesus' first words to them were, "Peace be with you!" (John 20:21). How do you think the disciples felt when they heard those words?

6. Try this experiment. Think of something you've done wrong—something you perhaps do not feel forgiven for doing. Now close your eyes and think of it in God's presence. Say aloud this paraphrase of 1 John 1:9: "In the name of Jesus Christ, I am forgiven." Sit quietly and soak in that. How does it feel to *truly know* you have been forgiven?

God's Forgiveness Flourishes in Us

People who are hard, unhappy, unloving, and unkind are often those who do not *feel* loved by God, even if they profess belief in Christ. They have never experienced the reality that God "freely give[s] us all things . . . [so] who shall separate us from the love of Christ?" (Romans 8:32, 35 NKJV). Like love, forgiveness becomes an active part of our lives because we are forgiven. It is God's generosity that enables us to be generous and forgive those who have offended us.

When we think of our sins and how unequal we are in light of God's standards of righteousness, our faith will not be capable of moving out and receiving cleansing from God unless we are standing in this mode of forgiveness. *Cleansed* is a lovely word. To cleanse something is to take the spot away; the dirt is removed. We can't even see where the spot was in the first place. So it's a matter of how we see ourselves—that we are cleansed. When we experience forgiveness, it becomes a way of life with which we learn to identify.

One reason we may still *feel* unclean after confessing our sins is because there is someone whom we have not forgiven. We all need to look deeply into our hearts and ask God if there is such a person whom we need to forgive. The connection between God forgiving us and us forgiving others is entwined with him living in us. As God increasingly occupies our hearts, we are able to forgive more. The experience of forgiveness comes to those who first forgive, just as there is a connection between the experience of being loved and being able to love.

As we learn to forgive, we *receive* forgiveness and enter into it as a way of life. We no longer hold those who have wronged us responsible in our thoughts or actions toward them or base our behavior toward them on what they have done—just as God does with us. We no longer blame them. We lay down the grudge. The *inward* side of forgiving means that we no longer brood or dwell on the hurt or wrong. We choose to forgive because we want to be involved with God's action. He is in the business of forgiveness, and therefore so are we.

7. Have an honest conversation with God about someone you struggle to forgive. (You might begin by asking, "How can I see this person as cleansed? Isn't that naive?") The purpose of this is not to get answers but to simply converse with your forgiving God. Write down your reflections on this time with God in the space below.

8. Now try this experiment. Think again of the person you struggle to forgive. Close your eyes and think of him or her in God's presence. Then say aloud this paraphrase of 1 John 1:9: "In the name of Jesus Christ, this person is forgiven." Sit quietly and soak in that. (If you wish, add, "Help me to forgive this person as well.") How do you think it would feel to truly release that person who wronged you? In what ways would it help *you*?

Forward Giving

Forgiveness can be viewed as "forward giving" in that it looks forward and envisions the future to be generous and giving. Forgiveness does not look backward—it does not hold on to the past or make the other person suffer because of the wrongs that he or she did. We have come to some degree of liberty from the hurt because we have *chosen* to look to the future.

"Forward giving" also means living in readiness to forgive, even toward a person who is unable to receive forgiveness from us. This works at the level of our will. Pain generally is like that: we have some degree of choice. We can either soak our mind in the pain or move forward with God toward healing. Forgiveness means we are not obsessed or dominated by the pain.

It is true that some wounds are so deep that we may hurt as a result of them for the rest of our lives. But as that pain mixes with our experience of life in the kingdom of God, we are not *consumed* by the pain, even though we remember it. We can still find joy and contentment in the eternal kind of life that God offers us.

It is not necessarily true that we haven't forgiven someone if we don't forget the harm done. We can still forgive them—no longer blaming them. Forgiveness does not mean to forget. Someone who has harmed us may say, "If you haven't stopped hurting, you haven't forgiven me." But this is not the case. Those who say such things may be trying to manipulate us because they are struggling to come to terms with what they have done.

Furthermore, the hurt we are feeling may go on even after we have let the other person "off the hook" and released our intention to pay him or her back. The mark of forgiveness is not that we no longer hurt. It is that we are no longer preoccupied with the hurt.

To be ready to forgive means that we are not surprised by the things people do that offend us: words said or not said, actions taken or not taken. We don't expect to be treated like royalty. Most humans think of themselves first—it is only by being immersed in the incredible love of God that it occurs to anyone to think of the other person first. But as we become "unoffendable," it becomes easier for us to think of others first. As the psalmist wrote, "Great peace have they which love thy law: and nothing shall offend them" (Psalm 119:165 KJV).

9. How can you live in a state of being "ready to forgive" (not being surprised when people hurt you) but still "envision the future to be generous and giving"?

10. What does it mean that the "mark" of forgiveness is not that you no longer hurt but that you are no longer preoccupied with the hurt? What are some healthy steps you can take when you sense that you are preoccupied with being hurt?

Responding to What Jesus Said

Where to Start

Many people *want* to forgive but are not sure *how*. Here are some ideas that may help you.

First, *be mindful that forgiveness is not a simple act of will*. If someone has hurt you badly, don't just try to not pay them back, but fill your mind with Jesus Christ and how he responded to those who hurt him. Dwell on stories of his life. Consider how he must have felt when he was wronged. This will immediately take you away from yourself and your injury, and it will put your mind in the right place to receive the grace of forgiveness.

Second, *admit that you cannot forgive without God's help*. Don't assume the burden of making forgiveness happen all on your own. Ask for God's grace to enter your heart and mind to help you. If you say to God, "I can't forgive," he will say to you, "Of course you can't forgive without my help." Forgiveness comes from God *through* you to others. Then, because Christ is living in you, you will be able to forgive those whom you thought you could never forgive.

Third, *realize that forgiving may take a while*. It may take a month or a few years. Sometimes, God may give you a gift of grace and take away the resentment and hurt, but generally, you cannot count on that. So pray for it, wait for it, and be persistent in asking.

Finally, *occasionally concentrate your thoughts and prayers—in manageable amounts—for the good of the individual who has hurt you*. Be careful not to put yourself in the role of being the one to straighten out the person's life. You are not his or her savior; Jesus Christ is his or her Savior. Try to simply come to where you can pray honestly for that person's good.

11. As Jesus hung on the cross, he was able to look at the soldiers who had nailed him there and say, "Father, forgive them, for they do not know what they do" (Luke 23:34 NKJV). He actually meant this because he had a heart practiced in forgiveness, and when he said those words, his heart was full of generosity toward them. He wasn't praying through gritted teeth in an effort to impress God; he genuinely wanted what was best for them. Take a moment to write down what you think and feel about this.

12. Reflect on each of the four ideas presented on how to forgive: (1) know that forgiveness is not just an act of will, (2) admit you cannot forgive without God's help, (3) realize that forgiving may take a while, and (4) occasionally concentrate your thoughts and prayers for the good of the offender. Which of these ideas is most helpful to you at this time? Why do you find that particular idea to be the most helpful?

Key Terms

Unforgiveness: Refusing to let an individual who has wronged you "off the hook" and instead seeking retribution and attempting to get even with that person. Unforgiveness is the way of normal life in this world and is deeply embedded into society's way of thinking.

Denarius: A common unit of money in Jesus' day. As noted in lesson 7, one talent was roughly equivalent to 6,000 denarii. In that time, a typical servant earned about one denarius a day. The unforgiving servant owed 10,000 talents to the king—so 60,000,000 times one day's wage.

For Further Reading

Everett L. Worthington Jr., *Forgiving and Reconciling: Bridges to Wholeness and Hope* (Lisle, IL: InterVarsity Press, 2003)

David Wenham, *The Parables of Jesus* (Lisle, IL: InterVarsity Press, 1989), chapter 8, about the Parable of the Unforgiving Servant.

Note

1. The unforgiving servant owed 10,000 talents to the king. One talent was equivalent to 6,000 denarii. In that time, a typical servant earned about one denarius a day.

LESSON 12

THE OUTRAGEOUS COMPASSION OF GOD

Parable of the Workers in the Vineyard (Matthew 20:1–16)

God's kingdom was so different from what people thought it would be that Jesus' listeners would have considered his ideas scandalous.

DALLAS WILLARD

The Parable of the Workers in the Vineyard clearly illustrates the Great Inversion we discussed in lesson 2. The landowner's act of paying the workers the same wage no matter how long they worked contradicted what was culturally acceptable (the way people generally thought about a situation) at the time and suggested another way of looking at things. Most cultures, both then and now, demand that people get exactly what they have earned for the hours they have worked. This is what they deserve—no more, no less. No doubt readers throughout the ages have wished this parable was not in the Bible. It still gets skipped over today. Admittedly, it is so counter to worldly wisdom that it appears outrageous.

If the parables were to derive their common titles from the hero of the story, this one would be called the Parable of the Compassionate Landowner or the Parable of the Compassionate Employer. The landowner seemed to understand that those who worked less weren't necessarily lazy, they were just without opportunity. He seemed to sense that all the workers wanted to work and needed to feed their families. So he paid them the same amount. Human justice isn't like that. Instead, those experiencing unemployment often feel hopeless in how their energy and talents are overlooked, while those who are employed judge those individuals to be idle.

Jesus was redefining justice through the landowner's actions. Justice means that God, as that landowner, shows compassion to all. He is glad to give people opportunities to do what they need to do to meet their needs. This was an extension of Jesus' idea that all are welcome in the kingdom. The person in charge (the landowner), as in many of Jesus' other parables (the forgiving king, the noble owner of the vineyard, the father of the prodigal), thought people really mattered and went many "extra miles" to give them opportunities.

Wise people in charge often understand this. For example, a young man was once convicted of a drug charge, for which the usual sentence was three years in a youth correctional facility. But the judge thought that he had not been challenged much in life and had been looking for an opportunity for adventure. So, at the sentencing, he gave the young man a choice: serve the three years in the youth correctional facility, or serve three years on a fishing boat off the Aleutian Islands in Alaska, working for the judge's friend who couldn't find good helpers. The young man chose the latter. He stayed on after three years, eventually becoming a partner in the fishing business and marrying the boss's daughter. According to the "normal" standards of justice, he didn't get what he deserved. But the judge gave him what he needed.

Kingdom justice does not suppose that justice is bereft of mercy. In the kingdom, mercy and justice are not opposites. No virtue, including justice, is without love, "which binds [all these virtues] in perfect unity" (Colossians 3:14).

1. Many people, like the older brother in the Parable of the Prodigal Son, resent God's kindness to those who haven't behaved properly. Why do you think this is the case?

2. Think about the judge's actions toward the young man convicted of a drug charge. When have you seen someone bend over backward to give an opportunity to someone?

Hearing What Jesus Said

The setting for the Parable of the Workers in the Vineyard is a conversation between Jesus and a man who is called the "rich young ruler" (see Matthew 19:16–22; Luke 18:18–23). In the midst of their discussion, Jesus told the man to give all his money to the poor and then come and follow him—that is, be his disciple. We can imagine the confused look on the faces of the disciples who, like the rest of their culture, thought this young man was more than acceptable *with* his riches. Their culture assumed that people with wealth had God's favor.

When the young man "went away sad, because he had great wealth" (Matthew 19:22), Jesus said to his disciples, "I tell you, it is easier for a camel to go through the eye of a needle than for someone who is rich to enter the kingdom of God" (Matthew 19:24). This prompted Peter to blurt out, "See, we have left all and followed You. Therefore what shall we have?" (Matthew 19:27 NKJV). Jesus told this parable as part of his response to that question:

"For the kingdom of heaven is like a landowner who went out early in the morning to hire laborers for his vineyard. Now when he had agreed with the laborers for a denarius a day, he sent them into his vineyard. And he went out about the third hour and saw others standing idle in the marketplace, and said to them, 'You also go into the vineyard, and whatever is right I will give you.' So they went. Again he went out about the sixth and the ninth hour, and did likewise. And about the eleventh hour he went out and found others standing idle, and said to them, 'Why have you been standing here idle all day?' They said to him, 'Because no one hired us.' He said to them, 'You also go into the vineyard, and whatever is right you will receive.'

"So when evening had come, the owner of the vineyard said to his steward, 'Call the laborers and give them their wages, beginning with the last to the first.' And when those came who were hired about the eleventh hour, they each received a denarius. But when the first came, they supposed that they would receive more; and they likewise received each a denarius. And when they had received it, they complained against the landowner, saying, 'These last men have worked only one hour, and you made them equal to us who have borne the burden and the heat of the day.' But he answered one of them and said, 'Friend, I am doing you no wrong. Did you not agree with me for a denarius? Take what is yours and go your way. I wish to give to this last man the same as to you. Is it not lawful for me to do what I wish with my own things? Or is your eye evil because I am good?' So the last will be first, and the first last. For many are called, but few chosen" (Matthew 20:1–16 NKJV).

The landowner went to the marketplace early in the morning (probably the equivalent to 6:00 AM) and found people waiting for jobs. The same thing still happens today—day laborers wait on selected street corners or in front of hardware stores, hoping that general contractors and farmers will stop by to hire them for the day. Apparently, this landowner needed more workers than he had anticipated, so he returned at 9:00 AM, and then at noon, and then at 3:00 PM. Each time he saw more workers waiting, so he hired them and told them they would be paid what was fair. When he came by at 5:00 PM, he was surprised to see workers still hoping to be hired. The text doesn't say he needed them, necessarily, but he hired them anyway.

This parable is bookended by Jesus' teaching that "many who are first will be last" (Matthew 19:30) and "the last will be first" (see Matthew 19:30; 20:16). Variations on this phrase occur eight times in the Gospels in different settings (see Matthew 12:45; 19:30; 20:16; Mark 9:35; 10:31; Luke 11:26; 13:30), so it is evident that this stands as a foundational teaching that the kingdom of God reverses the order that is present in human affairs.

3. Think of the many different characters in this parable: the landowner, the workers who started at different times—6:00 AM, 9:00 AM, noon, 3:00 PM, and 5:00 PM—and the workers who complained to the landowner. With whom do you most identify? Why?

4. Examine the landowner's response: "Friend, I am doing you no wrong. Did you not agree with me for a denarius? Take what is yours and go your way. I wish to give to this last man the same as to you. Is it not lawful for me to do what I wish with my own things? Or is your eye evil because I am good?" What reasons did he give the complainers?

Thinking About What Jesus Said

Redefining Justice

Suppose you were one of the laborers who started working at 6:00 AM. By the end of the day you would have been exhausted, worn out, and filthy. As you walked up to be paid, you may have thought, *I'm going to get paid more than the guys who got here later!* When you then discovered the landowner was paying every worker the same amount, you likely would have thought, *How can this be?* The workers who started early thought the same—and complained. Even though the owner had paid them exactly what he promised, they wanted more. The owner had disrupted their human sense of fairness by paying everyone the full day's wage.

Dallas Willard told of how he had worked as a migrant field-worker. He had experienced what it is like to stand on the street corner and hope that someone chose him for a job.[1] We have to have sympathy for such workers, especially for those like the men in the parable who had been waiting all day. By 4:30 PM, they still hadn't gotten any work. Perhaps they thought about their children at home who didn't have food. They needed to work! Work gives us a place in life, a supply of resources, even if it's only for a day. The vineyard owner understood this.

In God's kingdom, fairness isn't really fair without love. Justice without love will never do justice to justice. In other words, justice that is stripped of love and mercy lacks true integrity, true decency, and true morality. The workers who didn't get hired until later in the day wanted to work, hoped to work, and waited to work. Their children were no less hungry than the children of the laborers who had worked all day. The workers who were hired late received the sort of justice found only in the upside-down kingdom of God. Love and mercy permeate God's kingdom, and this then naturally takes care of justice as well.

Love, however, must not be confused with constantly doing for others what they can do for themselves. In the New Testament, the Greek word used for the type of love that God wants his followers to show to others is *agape*. This kind of love—*agape* love—does what is best for the other person, which may not be what he or she wants or even demands. The landowner didn't give the 5:00 PM workers something for nothing; he didn't hire them because he felt guilty or pushed. *Agape* love doesn't enable another person to be irresponsible.

Demonstrating *agape* love—doing what is best for the other person—motivates us to help others move forward, gives them opportunities to flourish, and even sees in them what they may not see in themselves.

5. Why does true justice absolutely require that love exists at its core?

6. What would kingdom justice infused with *agape* love look like in government, or in business, or in church life, or in school?

The Generosity of Justice

As noted previously, most cultures today expect people to get compensated for the work they perform, and people are resentful when that doesn't happen. However, the nature of the kingdom of God is not based on exact compensation but on giving to those in need. It is much like Jesus said about dinner guests: "But when you give a feast, invite the poor, the maimed, the lame, the blind. And you will be blessed, because they cannot repay you; for you shall be repaid at the resurrection of the just" (Luke 14:13–14 NKJV).

On December 11, 1995, Malden Mills, a textile factory in Massachusetts, burned to the ground. When this happened, some people probably thought, *This is a great opportunity for the owner. He can collect on his insurance, build a factory where it's cheaper, and then live off the money and make a lot more money*. However, the owner, Aaron Feuerstein, kept paying the 1,400 employees of the factory who were suddenly out of work. He kept paying them until a new factory was built and even allowed them to keep their benefits. Feuerstein was quoted as saying, "I'm not throwing 3,000 people out of work two weeks before Christmas."[2]

Many people thought Feuerstein was a fool, but he was simply a good man. He wasn't thinking about how to take advantage of the situation. He was thinking about the welfare of the people who worked for him. Many business owners who are like Feuerstein also recognize the responsibility they have toward their workers and respond to it. They set aside the worldly wisdom of what others think they should do and just do the right thing.

John Ruskin, a philosopher and art critic of the Victorian era, wrote that the merchant or manufacturer's role was to provide work for people, not just make a profit. Business owners were not to focus on making products as cheaply as possible but to create work that benefited both buyers and employees.[3] This wisdom combines skill and intelligence with kindness. It resembles Paul's admonition to "do nothing out of selfish ambition or vain conceit . . . not looking to your own interests but each of you to the interests of the others" (Philippians 2:3–4).

7. How do you think the employees responded to Feuerstein's decision—in the moment, when they returned to work, and in their treatment of others?

8. If someone defended his or her profit-focused practices by saying, "business is business," how might you respond without being preachy?

The Effect of Comparison

Notice how Jesus crafted the Parable of the Workers in the Vineyard by having the landowner pay the workers in the reverse order in which they were hired. By paying the 5:00 PM workers first, the people who started early in the morning got to watch and anticipate being paid more than the agreed-upon amount. At the end when they complained about not being paid more, the landowner pointed out that they had agreed to the fair and adequate wage that he had paid them. He continued, "Take your pay and go. I want to give the one who was hired last the same as I gave you. Don't I have the right to do what I want with my own money? Or are you envious because I am generous?" (Matthew 20:14–15). Leaving the story open-ended allowed people to keep thinking, *What would I have done in those circumstances?*

The earliest workers found fault with the landowner not because they were inadequately paid but because of what they were paid in *comparison* to others. If they had not made that comparison, they might have gone home thinking, *I am so thankful that I got this job today!* But their comparison resulted in resentment instead of gratitude.

The effect of comparison is rarely good; in fact, it's usually destructive. People who have enough or who are well-off are generally grateful. But when they see others who are *better* off, they can suddenly feel that they are not so well-off after all.

Comparison, and its effect of envy, poisons our ideas of justice. In the Gospels, we read how the religious authorities' envy of Jesus caused them to ultimately hand him over to Pilate, the Roman governor. Pilate recognized they were doing this out of their own self-interests (see Matthew 27:18; Mark 15:10). They were well-off and well-positioned, but they couldn't perform miracles or healings, and they couldn't earn the respect of people, all of which Jesus could do. This comparison is what led them to plot how to kill Jesus.

The kingdom of God is a place where we can live indifferent to comparisons. It is a place where we can see our blessings in light of *God's* goodness to us, not in light of how they compare with *others'* blessings. In the kingdom of God, the hungry are filled and those who weep will laugh (see Luke 6:20–21). All are well-off in God's kingdom.

9. What enables a person to "live indifferent to comparisons" so that they don't even come to mind? What freedom is available to those who learn to live this way?

10. When you start making comparisons, what might you choose to think about instead?

Responding to What Jesus Said

Extending Grace to Others

The Parable of the Workers in the Vineyard shows that God is not stingy with his grace. It reveals that *all* service matters to him, even if it is small in comparison to the service of others. The parable also demonstrates how easily we can slip into a frame of mind like Peter had when he asked Jesus what he and the other disciples would receive after all their sacrifices.

It has been speculated that Jesus' repetition of the phrase "the first will be last and the last will be first" was a warning to the disciples. In the future, when all kinds of people joined the church after the Day of Pentecost, they might look back and see themselves as "first" because they were the first to walk with Christ. Jesus was saying that their time with him didn't put them at the head of the pecking order in God's sight. Similarly, those who serve in ways deemed significant can easily slip into thinking of themselves as being in God's "inner circle." In reality, God is out in the marketplace looking for people whom everyone else has ignored.

There is another caution we can take away from Peter's question to Jesus about what he and the other disciples would get out of their great sacrifice. When tragedies happen to devoted Christians, they may be tempted to wonder, *Why did this tragedy happen to me? I've done so much for God.* They never had these thoughts before the tragedy occurred, but now they find these thoughts slowly creeping into their thinking.

The truth is that we can bargain for God's grace. Our devotion or service to him doesn't entitle us to a so-called happy life. Our job—and privilege—is to partner with the Lord out in the marketplace, welcoming strangers and being open to new believers in the church fellowship . . . and even a new pastor with whom we don't agree. The true answer to Peter's question of what we "get" is the joy of working, serving, and partnering with God.

11. Who might be considered "last" in your community? In your church? In your family? Why do you think that particular person is considered last?

12. Think of someone you know who is considered "last" in this way. Picture him or her, and then ask God, "What does this person need most? What do they need most from me?" Write down any thoughts or reflections that you receive after doing this.

Key Term

***Agape*:** A Greek term often used in the New Testament to describe the kind of love that is of God and from God (see John 3:16). This kind of love does what is in the best interests of the other person, which may not be what he or she wants or even demands. *Agape* is distinguished from *philia,* another word in the New Testament translated as "love," which refers to a kind of brotherly love between close friends (see Romans 12:10). Two other Greek words translated as "love" that do not appear in the New Testament include *storge,* a type of strong love between family members, and *eros,* the type of love found in romantic relationships.[4]

For Further Reading

Dallas Willard, *Knowing Christ Today: Why We Can Trust Spiritual Knowledge* (San Francisco: HarperOne, 2009), chapter 3, about justice and love.

Kenneth Bailey, *Jesus Through Middle Eastern Eyes: Cultural Studies in the Gospels* (Lisle, IL: InterVarsity Press, 2008), chapter 28.

Notes

1. Willard, *The Scandal of the Kingdom*, 196.
2. "Back from the Ashes," *Hartford Courant*, November 13, 2005, https://www.courant.com/2005/11/13/back-from-the-ashes-2/.
3. John Ruskin, "Unto This Last," quoted in Dallas Willard, *Called to Business* (Willard Family Trust, 2018), 39.
4. Robert H. Mounce, *John,* in *The Expositor's Bible Commentary,* vol. 10 (Grand Rapids, MI: Zondervan Academic, 2007), commentary on John 3:16, 400.

LESSON 13

WHAT IS YOUR LIFE: RICHES IN THE KINGDOM

Parable of the Foolish Rich Farmer (Luke 12:16–21)

The answer to the question, "What is your life" is not found in riches or possessions or gain, but can only be found in a heart that fully trusts God.

DALLAS WILLARD

The situation that prompted Jesus to tell the Parable of the Foolish Rich Farmer was a request that a man in the crowd made to him: "Teacher, tell my brother to divide the inheritance with me" (Luke 12:13). Jesus' response to the man was as countercultural as ever: "Man, who appointed me a judge or an arbiter between you? . . . Be on your guard against all kinds of greed" (Luke 12:14–15). Jesus' warning to the man to guard himself against *the spirit of always wanting more* was the opposite of what any so-called successful culture believed.

Most cultures promote the idea that people should set higher and higher goals for themselves, especially when it comes to accumulating possessions. They should earn more this year than they did last year. They should move up to a larger living space with more room. They should want their children to have more than they had growing up. *More* is somehow better—more possessions, more income, more status.

Sometimes, *having more* is a good idea. But *chasing more* never is. God's creation is full of beauty, and he loves to give good gifts. As we grow toward God, we want to be as generous as he is. The problem arises when the thought of having more preoccupies us. The issue is not the possession of those things but the effect it has on us when we treasure them in our hearts.

The Parable of the Foolish Rich Farmer is thus about our relationship to riches and guarding against "all kinds of greed" (Luke 12:15). The farmer in the story wasn't foolish because he was rich but because his riches were his treasure. Wealth can deceive us, "choke the word," and cause us to become "unfruitful" for God (see Matthew 13:22), because we become preoccupied with doing whatever it takes to reach goals centered on accumulation. We don't think about or enjoy what it means to be "rich toward God" (Luke 12:21).

Jesus' interaction with the man in the crowd resembles his interaction with the rich young ruler. As discussed in lesson 12, Jesus wanted that man to be his disciple but said he first had to sell all he had—and then he would have treasure in heaven (see Matthew 19:21). Apparently, Jesus could see that the man's possessions were the center of his world. Jesus was good at getting to the heart of who people really were and what their lives were all about.

This is the issue that Jesus points out in the Parable of the Foolish Rich Farmer: the "deceitfulness" of riches (see Matthew 13:22; Mark 4:19). This deception is about being hooked on "gain" and always wanting to have more. No matter how much or how little we have, it often feels like "the grass is greener" on the other side of the fence. It's impossible to know if that is true, of course, but still, we compare and speculate about how much better things would be if we had more or had something better or different.

If we have a right heart about money, it will help us avoid all kinds of problems—credit card debt, get-rich-quick schemes, taking advantage of others, getting loans from others, and the worry that accompanies these things. What is that right heart about money? *All* material things belong to God: "The earth is the

LORD's, and everything in it" (Psalm 24:1). Money is a blessing from God that we are to manage in light of loving God with all our heart and loving others as ourselves. Like Abraham, we are blessed to be a blessing to others (see Genesis 12:3).

1. When is having a higher goal a good idea—and when is it not?

2. What are some other problems in life that might stem from money issues?

Hearing What Jesus Said

As just noted, Jesus told the Parable of the Foolish Rich Farmer to address the ever-present desire that people have to possess more and more.

> Then He spoke a parable to them, saying: "The ground of a certain rich man yielded plentifully. And he thought within himself, saying, 'What shall I do, since I have no room to store my crops?' So he said, 'I will do this: I will pull down my barns and build greater, and there I will store all my crops and my goods'" (Luke 12:16–18 NKJV).

At this point, the farmer, who was already rich, was being sensible and trying to manage his enormous crop. But he made a mistake in his next breath, believing that what his life was really about was the abundance of what he possessed. The farmer figured that the wealth that came to him was for no other purpose than to make himself comfortable, which seemed to be the goal of his life.

> "And I will say to my soul, 'Soul, you have many goods laid up for many years; take your ease; eat, drink, and be merry'" (Luke 12:19 NKJV).

Talking to one's soul is a good thing to do. In fact, the psalmists did this many times (see, for example, Psalms 43:5; 57:8; 62:5; 103:1; 116:7). Talking to our soul expresses what we are really thinking. The farmer's plans to eat, drink, and be merry were fine. Jesus himself did that. It was also good for his soul to be at rest—except for what it was resting in. The problem was that he was making riches and leisure the idols and the essence of his life.

As the farmer spoke to his soul, God interrupted and focused directly on his character:

> "But God said to him, 'Fool! This night your soul will be required of you; then whose will those things be which you have provided?' So is he who lays up treasure for himself, and is not rich toward God" (Luke 12:20–21 NKJV).

The rich man made the mistake of abandoning the maker of his soul and laying up treasure for himself in external things. He was not rich toward God, who had provided those blessings to him (see Luke 12:21). His story illustrates the opposite of what it means to see ourselves as "foreigners and exiles" on this earth and abstain from giving into "sinful desires, which wage war against your soul" (1 Peter 2:11). The rich man never saw beyond himself or this world. Instead of denying himself, he aggressively gathered more for himself and held on to it. Instead of finding joy in *giving*, he found joy in *keeping*.

3. What are some things the farmer in this parable might have said to his soul if he had been "rich toward God"?

4. What is the difference between managing our wealth and possessions sensibly and those things being the "essence" of our lives?

Thinking About What Jesus Said

Greed as a Form of Idolatry

Remember that Jesus was prompted to offer this parable in response to a man's plea that he tell his brother to share the inheritance with him. The man was probably a younger son whose older brother had received the family inheritance but wasn't forthcoming in sharing it. People often approached rabbis with family disputes, and this young man probably saw how Jesus spoke with authority and thought that he could solve his problem. So the young man asked Jesus to tell his brother to divide the inheritance, implying, "So I can get what I want."

Jesus sidestepped the young man's directive and posed a different agenda, telling him to be on guard against "all kinds of greed" (Luke 12:15). Jesus apparently saw into this young man's heart and knew the first step in solving his problem was to address his desire for money. The man needed to be reconciled to his brother, and sharing the inheritance was a part of that.

Notice that Jesus spoke of *all kinds* of greed. What other kinds of greed are there besides wanting more *wealth* or *possessions*? Anytime we want more than our fair share of *anything*, greed may be involved: wanting more than our share of attention, wanting more than our share of gifts from others, wanting to receive more praise or respect than is due to us. Greed is a disease of the self—being overly conscious of everything related to the self—which naturally makes it difficult to love God and others wholeheartedly.

Covetousness is a form of greed that focuses on wanting what another person has. This young man was being eaten up by wanting what his brother had: access to the inheritance. Paul said that the disease of greed is in fact idolatry (see Colossians 3:5). What we want becomes an idol because we believe it will solve our problems, and we will do anything we can to get it.

As with all idols, this one must be eliminated and replaced by true goodness: *gratitude*. In gratitude, we stop thinking about whatever it is we so obsessively want and become glad that God provides what we need—and, in many cases, what we simply want. While greed brings enslavement to getting what we want, gratitude creates freedom to enjoy what we have.

5. What are some of the forms that greed takes in your life? In other words, what are some of the things that you are often tempted to become greedy about in your life?

6. Greed brings enslavement to getting what you want while gratitude creates freedom to enjoy what you have. What other ways is life better lived in gratitude than in greed?

Setting Our Heart on God

Deep soul-searching is required when we explore the problem of being devoted to having more. The rich farmer's delusion was that his life consisted of enjoying his success, taking his rest, and trusting in his goods. Jesus offered this diagnosis: "So is he who lays up treasure for himself, and is not rich toward God" (Luke 12:21 NKJV).

This parable isn't about being rich but about the way we hold the wealth we do have or wish for what we don't have. The farmer held his crops as if they were his own, but he was mistaken. He didn't produce his bumper crop; the "ground" did, as Jesus was careful to say (see Luke 12:16). He thought he was entirely in control of it, and so he laid up treasures for himself.

So, how can we know whether we are laying up treasures for ourselves or are rich toward God? One of the best ways to figure this out is to work on this question: *With what are our thoughts, feelings, and desires preoccupied?* Our life is that to which we devote our time, our energy, our thoughts. It is what, as Jesus said, we have set our hearts on. "For where your treasure is, there your heart will be also" (Matthew 6:21).

Often, we can detect what we treasure the most by what we count on to give us security—national security, Social Security, insurance, bank accounts, even key relationships. This is a reflection of the fact that human life is *in*secure apart from God. To be "rich toward God" is to live in the reality that our only security is in God and everything else is just a prop. To live in God's security is to be immersed in the truth that God lavishes his love on us and will guide us through both our trials and our exciting adventures of life.

It's a life of interaction with God, who wants to dwell in us. We can be secure because we live in the unshakable kingdom of God. Yes, we may go through very difficult times, but God can redeem any destructive thing that happens to us. We are never alone, never forsaken. Never. The "barns" where we store our "riches" are only a part of our life because our life is an *eternal* kind of life—one lived in reliance on the resources of the kingdom of God.[1]

7. Take a few moments to pause and ask God what are the three most common things you focus on during moments of free time such as driving, cleaning, or fixing things. Simply notice without judgment and write them down in the space below. Look at this list again tomorrow and adjust any items you wrote down as needed. When you are ready, ask God to show you what you need to know about each of these things.

8. What has helped you the most in your life to move toward being "rich toward God"?

Eternal Kind of Gain

Having more does not make us content. On the contrary, continually thinking "I gotta have more" makes us restless and crabby. In truth, godliness—life with God and from him—is great gain and brings deep satisfaction. As the apostle Paul wrote, trying to get rich is full of traps and creates reckless, unwise desires that plunge us into stress and ruin (see 1 Timothy 6:6–9).

Paul went so far as to say that "the love of money is a root of all kinds of evil" (1 Timothy 6:10). It will pierce us with many sorrows. Our best course of action is thus to avoid activities and even people who are focused on such pursuits. We can replace this with putting our energy and desires toward becoming a disciple of Jesus, taking the time to wonder how he would live our life if he were in our situation.

Jesus practiced simplicity of life, owning little and relying on God to provide. We can do the same by owning less, spending less, and hurrying less. Owning less creates a certain detachment from possessions and helps us see ourselves as managers of the possessions God has given us rather than avid collectors of the newest merchandise. With less mental clutter—remembering where we've put everything that we have come to possess—we have mental space to pursue faith, love, patience, goodness, and gentleness (see 1 Timothy 6:11).

Paul went on to give instructions to the "rich of this world." When you consider the economic status of most of the people in the world, those who live in developed countries fit in the category of the "rich of this world." Paul instructs this group as follows:

> Command those who are rich in this present world not to be arrogant nor to put their hope in wealth, which is so uncertain, but to put their

> hope in God, who richly provides us with everything for our enjoyment. Command them to do good, to be rich in good deeds, and to be generous and willing to share. In this way they will lay up treasure for themselves as a firm foundation for the coming age, so that they may take hold of the life that is truly life (1 Timothy 6:17–19).

Another part of our discipleship is to be "rich in good deeds." When God gave Abraham a vision for his people, he promised that he would bless Abraham and that, in turn, all nations of the earth would be blessed (see Genesis 12:3). We are blessed to be a blessing to others. An unusual influx of cash is not a time to think about what we can buy but whom we might bless.

9. Picture in your mind an altar where your house, your bank account, and all your possessions sit. Think about the idea that "the earth is the LORD's, and everything in it" (Psalm 24:1). Consider that God owns your coffeepot as well as the bed in which you sleep—and take joy in that fact. Thank God for all these things. Then, if you are willing, ask God to reveal how you might bless others through his possessions that are in your care. Write what he brings to your mind in the space below.

10. Who do you know who is "rich in good deeds"? How would you describe that person and the life that he or she leads? What about that peson do you most admire?

Responding to What Jesus Said

Investing in People

John Wesley believed in *saving all you can* and *giving all you can*.[2] Dallas Willard liked to insert *using all you can* in between them. We are to use what we have to take care of all that we have been given in a way that would please God. We can take possession of property to use for the glory of God as well as our own enjoyment of life before God. We can talk with God about our monetary decisions (houses, cars, stocks, tithing, clothing, entertainment, helping those in need) so that those decisions flow out of our discipleship to him, asking, *How would Jesus live his life if he were me? If he had a big backyard? If he had a car that ran well?*

When Jesus once taught about worry, he said this odd thing: "Provide purses for yourselves that will not wear out, a treasure in heaven that will never fail" (Luke 12:33). Other translations say "moneybags that do not grow old" (ESV). Those everlasting purses or moneybags that continue into eternity are *people*—others and ourselves. Humans have an eternal life, and we invest in people and their character with teaching, conversations, and good deeds. The difference we make in the lives of other people will go to heaven when *they* go to heaven. Anything we do for someone else remains for eternity.

People are what matter. They are the temple of God. They are God's chosen out of the world. They are his bride. What we can do for others, especially for "the least of these my brethren" (Matthew 25:40 KJV)—that is the treasure that has gone on to heaven.

11. Name four people who have invested in you besides your parents. Perhaps they didn't realize they were doing so—it's just how they were with people. Beside each person's name, write down one investment they made in you that especially stands out.

12. Now take a moment to ponder who God might want *you* to invest in with your time, energy, encouragement, or financial resources. Beside each person's name, write down one way that you could invest in him or her. (You may want to take a look at your list of contacts or an address book. See what comes to you a few hours or days later.)

Key Terms

Wealth: Your accumulated resources and assets, which can be measured in terms of either real goods or money value; any skills or talents you use to make a living are part of your wealth.

Greed: A desire to acquire more that is to be avoided. Jesus said, "Be on your guard against all kinds of greed; life does not consist in an abundance of possessions" (Luke 12:15). Paul wrote that "the love of money [greed] is a root of all kinds of evil" (1 Timothy 6:10).

For Further Reading

David Wenham, *The Parables of Jesus* (Lisle, IL: InterVarsity Press, 1989), chapter 7 about the Parable of the Foolish Rich Farmer.

Jan Johnson, *Abundant Simplicity: Discovering Unhurried Rhythms of Grace* (Lisle, IL: InterVarsity Press, 2011), about living with God in a spirit of frugality and letting go of owning and acquiring (so many!) possessions.

Notes

1. Adapted from Dallas Willard, "How God Is in Business," Macon Bible Institute audio series, session 5, First Presbyterian Church, Macon, GA, August 2001, published in Willard, *Called to Business*, 9–25.
2. William Barclay, *The Daily Bible Study Series: The Gospel of Luke* (Philadelphia: Westminster Press, 1956), 168.

LESSON 14

PERSISTENCE AS THE PREREQUISITE TO GROWTH

Illustration of the Master and the Servant, Parable of the Widow and the Mean Judge, and Parable of the Pharisee and the Tax Collector (Luke 17:3–10; 18:1–17)

Life in the kingdom goes beyond the minimum.

DALLAS WILLARD

Think of some people in your life who are calm, steady, and stable. What is it like to work with them? Most likely, they are people you can count on because they follow through. You know they are in it for the "long haul" and are going to be around tomorrow. They are resilient and bounce back easily. They just keep on going, no matter what.

This is the kind of persistence that Jesus described in the parables we will discuss in this lesson: *quiet* yet *diligent*. On the one hand, persistence doesn't make a lot of noise; on the other hand, it is determined and tough. But most of all, persistence is never anxious and never quits. When we think of a person who is *persistent*—perhaps because the word *persistent* itself sounds a bit like the word *pest*—we may think of someone who nags, annoys, or talks too loudly. However, while persistence is active, not passive, it's the kind of strong activity that doesn't draw attention to itself. We can count on a person who possesses this kind of persistence.

The abundant life that Jesus came to give us is a gift (see John 10:10), but we still have to take the initiative to receive it and to walk into it. God's grace expands when the recipient of the gift cooperates with God's empowerment. To "grow in the grace and knowledge of our Lord and Savior Jesus Christ" (2 Peter 3:18) involves continuing, well-directed action. We need *persistence*: the will to consistently stick to and apply the means to our goal. We need *patience*: a willingness to let the life we are living grow and to take the wise course of action. And we need *confidence* that the Holy Spirit will do this in us as we cooperate.

This kind of cooperation is full of energy! Jesus said, "Strive to enter through the narrow gate" (Luke 13:24 NKJV). To strive means to put our total attention into what we and God are "doing together" early in the day and throughout the day. To strive indicates that our faith is a whole-life activity, because God is interested in our whole life: our work and what it means to us; our leisure (yes, including watching football) and how it renews us; our relationships and how they form us. In other words, faith is not a sideline interest to dabble in on Sundays or an occasional pastime we are good at (like taking a class or filling in this workbook!).

God's grace empowers us in our spiritual growth as we respond with planned, determined effort. It's long-term, like running a marathon. It's short-term, like the final few seconds of a championship basketball game. The parables in this lesson highlight four key areas where persistent diligence is especially needed: service, forgiveness, prayer, and humility. Our persistent efforts to forgive freely, serve wholeheartedly, pray unceasingly, and humbly regard others as better than ourselves will increase our faith, confidence, and dependence on God.

1. What do you find to be helpful about a person who acts with quiet persistence? Why might you want to be friends with that person or work with that person?

2. Who have you known who exhibits the quality of quiet persistence? What was it about that person's life that especially stood out to you?

Hearing What Jesus Said

In the Illustration of the Master and the Servant, Jesus offered a picture of quiet diligence as a servant taking initiative without being told what to do or waiting to be thanked. In Jesus' day, servants did their jobs without reminders or nagging. It was also the custom to never thank a servant, even one who worked all day in the field, cleaned up, and served the food.

> "And which of you, having a servant plowing or tending sheep, will say to him when he has come in from the field, 'Come at once and sit down to eat'? But will he not rather say to him, 'Prepare something for my supper, and gird yourself and serve me till I have eaten and drunk, and afterward you will eat and drink'? Does he thank that servant because he did the things that were commanded him? I think not" (Luke 17:7–9 NKJV).

Sluggish, half-hearted servants thought, *I did what I was told to do. There's nothing more to be done.* They had little regard for their work and never thought about what more they could do to contribute to the household's efficiency and satisfaction. They did their duty but went no further. Purposeful and dependable servants, on the other hand, worked diligently without needing to be told what to do, and they did so without fanfare. They expected no congratulations. A master of the household might think (but never say), *My servants really identify with me and what I need. I wish I could hire workers like this in my business.*

Jesus went on to state that these servants labeled themselves as "unprofitable" (see Luke 17:10). However, in reality they were the best of workers: wholeheartedly going the extra mile in making the household run well. They were actually *profitable* servants, who then profited from their master's good pleasure. Such servants went beyond what was expected of them because *their whole heart was in what they did.*

> "So likewise you, when you have done all those things which you are commanded, say, 'We are unprofitable servants. We have done what was our duty to do'" (Luke 17:10 NKJV).

Likewise, in our life with God, we don't settle for thinking, *I did what I was told to do. There' s nothing more to be done.* Instead, we identify with God's love for people and go the extra mile in showing that love to them. We don't wait to step forward to do his work but take the initative. And we live our lives from the abundant reality of the kingdom of God, things such as forgiveness and service become natural for us. This is what life in the kingdom of God is like.

3. What causes a person to be willing—perhaps even eager—to go the extra mile for others? What motivates *you* to go the extra mile for others?

4. How would you describe the "interests of the master" in terms of what God is interested in doing in this world (at least with which you can identify)?

Thinking About What Jesus Said

Diligent in Forgiveness

The disciples had been taught they had to forgive someone who offended them. If that person offended them twice in one day, they may have considered themselves bighearted by forgiving that same offense twice in one day. So imagine how they felt when Jesus said, "Even if they sin against you *seven times in a day* and seven times come back to you saying 'I repent,' you must forgive them" (Luke 17:4, emphasis added). It is hard to conceive of forgiving someone who has called us a derogatory name or does something else to offend us seven times in one day!

But Jesus' outlandish declaration was for us to forgive the same offense again and again, no matter what. Even if the person is insincere, we still forgive. Jesus wants us to set ourselves up to forgive endlessly. The reason is simple: it is how God forgives us each day. Besides, loving people is better than becoming bitter toward them. *Life in the kingdom of God goes beyond the minimum* and instead participates in the abounding generosity of God.

The astounded disciples were certain this much forgiveness was impossible, so they replied, "Increase our faith!" (Luke 17:5). They knew it would take enormous confidence in God to let others' offenses go and rest in God's abundant protection. Otherwise, the alternate option was for them to tell the person, "You've exceeded your quota of two forgivable offenses a day. I can trust God only that far." The same is true in our lives.

Jesus seemed to understand their difficulty, which is why he then gave them the Illustration of the Master and the Servant, in which the diligent servant was gung-ho in going beyond the minimum because he identified with the master's purposes. In the same way, we must be diligent in going beyond the mininum when it comes to forgiving others. We can ask for grace ("increase our faith") to see what God is up to in the life of the person giving offense and reflect on how the Lord is inviting us to partner with him for that person's transformation.

5. How do you typically respond when you see someone committing the same offense repeatedly in the same week (or even in the same day)? What do you think you would say to God if those repeated offenses were made against you?

6. How have you seen that life is better if you can (through the power of the Spirit) forgive and let go? What would it take for you to forgive others the way that God forgives you?

Diligent in Prayer

The next story from Jesus in Luke's narrative, the Parable of the Widow and the Mean Judge, features a diligent and persevering woman. This persistent woman, who was a widow, didn't "lose heart" or give up even when facing a "judge who neither feared God nor cared what people thought" (Luke 18:2). This judge appears to have been more like a crime boss than a servant of justice. He had no respect for other people or for God. The widow may have known this but still pleaded with him, "Grant me justice against my adversary" (Luke 18:3).

In those days, widows were often helpless in society. People pushed them around because they didn't have a husband to defend them. They had no rights. So, this widow could only *ask* for justice because someone had taken advantage of her, possibly stealing from her.

For some time, the judge refused to help her. But he finally said to himself, "Even though I don't fear God or care what people think, yet because this widow keeps bothering me, I will see that she gets justice, so that she won't eventually come and attack me!" (Luke 18:4–5). The judge was probably not afraid of her but was tired that she kept coming.

In this parable, Jesus borrowed from a well-known tendency in people to give in when someone keeps coming to them with a request. It's why we may cross the street or avoid making eye contact with someone who is asking for money or other resources—we don't want to feel that tug to give. We can become overwhelmed by the power of someone's request and give in because asking and giving come from the deepest parts of human nature.

Jesus used this tendency in humans to urge us to continue praying for our requests. We are not to quit or give up in our interaction with God. Just engaging in conversation with him is in itself a way to not lose heart, and often our request will change and mature in the midst of our ongoing conversation. We find peace in knowing that we are never alone and that the Creator of the universe is watching out for us. We pray not out of duty but out of relationship; not out of obedience but out of love. As our faith grows, so does our desire to speak with God.

7. Some people misinterpret the Parable of the Widow and the Mean Judge in Luke 18:1–8 to mean that God is like the unjust judge—not ready to hear us and wanting us to exhaust ourselves. How is God's posture toward hearing from us very different?

8. Jesus understood the transformation that comes into our lives when we engage with God in consistent and ongoing prayer. In your life, when you have prayed for something over a long period of time, what do you find happens within *you*?

Diligent in Humility

Jesus concluded this teaching in Luke's narrative with a parable about humility and prayer. How is humility connected to prayer? Pride often keeps us from praying. If the widow who went to court had been self-important, she wouldn't have kept approaching the judge for help. She would have thought, *I won't approach him! He treats me as if I were nothing!*

Humility is about dependence on God. Sometimes we don't pray because we think we can work things out on our own rather than rely on God. We trust in ourselves, as did some of Jesus' listeners, who were "confident of their own righteousness and looked down on everyone else" (Luke 18:9). Jesus illustrated the problem with this way of thinking by telling the Parable of the Pharisee and the Tax Collector, in which he contrasted the prayer of a Pharisee with that of a tax collector. Jesus was familiar with both, having eaten with tax collectors who were despised political appointees of Rome and were normally corrupt in their business dealings.

> Jesus told this parable: "Two men went up to the temple to pray, one a Pharisee and the other a tax collector. The Pharisee stood by himself and prayed: 'God, I thank you that I am not like other people—robbers, evildoers, adulterers—or even like this tax collector. I fast twice a week and give a tenth of all I get.' But the tax collector stood at a distance. He would not even look up to heaven, but beat his breast and said, 'God, have mercy on me, a sinner'" (Luke 18:9–13).

Perhaps the Pharisee saw the tax collector pounding his chest in heartbreak and humility, asking only that God be merciful to him. This led the Pharisee to speak of how good he was, mentioning his strict spiritual practices. Simply asking God for what he needed wasn't impressive enough. Jesus' response to the prayers of the two men was the opposite of what the disciples expected: "I tell you that this man, rather than the other, went home justified before God." Jesus then offered a version of his "first shall be last" wisdom: "For all those who exalt themselves will be humbled, and those who humble themselves will be exalted" (Luke 18:14).

Humility enables us to get out of the way and connect with God. Humility is not thinking less of ourselves but thinking of ourselves less: "Let each think of the other better than themselves" (Philippians 2:3, paraphrase). How can we do this?

By seeing how Christ is remaking others. When we see in them what Christ can be, we are in a position to think better of them than ourselves. We are in a place where we are not thinking about ourselves at all! This is especially true because we know we are always thought of by God and he is taking care of us.

9. Think about these ideas regarding humility: (1) humility is about dependence on God, (2) humility is not thinking less of yourself but thinking of yourself less, and (3) humility leads you to a place where you actually think better of others than yourself because you see how Christ is remaking them. Which of these ideas stands out to you the most? Which makes humility seem less complicated and more doable in our relationships?

10. What is Jesus' promise in Luke 18:14 for those who humble themselves? How can living in the knowledge that you are "always thought of by God" and that "he is taking caring of you" equip you to genuinely rejoice with those who experience success?

Responding to What Jesus Said

Free-Hearted Collaboration with Jesus

As mentioned in lesson 3, God has no interest in creating religious robots. Instead, he desires us to be his colaborers and friends (see 2 Corinthians 6:1; James 2:23). As we grow in quiet diligence and intentionality, we have conversations with

God about what we want to do *and* his purposes for our lives. This wholehearted focus makes life interesting and adventurous—no more half-hearted living of chasing temptations and trying to make other people like us.

Being a disciple of Christ is not a matter of always asking, "What would Jesus do?" As we come to know Jesus and his ways, our experiential knowledge of him allows us to *recognize* what we need to do—at least in most cases. Dallas Willard likened this to how he didn't need to ask his wife, Jane, what she wanted or what she regarded as good because they had spent most of their lives together. It is our life together with Jesus in his kingdom that enables us to better understand what we are supposed to be doing. Paul prayed, "I want to know Christ" (Philippians 3:10), and, as we get to know him, he speaks in our hearts.

Being diligent in *service* creates a habit of going the extra mile to please God. Being diligent in *forgiveness* creates freedom from bitterness so that we are trustworthy in making decisions. Being diligent in *prayer* makes us into the kind of people who seek God. Being diligent in *humility* forms us into people who trust God in everything and depend on him. God helps people like this to mature by allowing them to make their own choices based on their deepening relationship with him. They become so close to him that they are engaged in free-hearted collaboration with Jesus and his friends in the kingdom.

11. Pause for a moment to think about these two phrases: (1) wholehearted collaboration with God, and (2) being a colaborer and friend of God. How does someone living this way have a different kind of life?

12. Choose one area in which you feel led to collaborate more closely with God: forgiving *freely*, serving *wholeheartedly*, praying *unceasingly*, and *humbly* regarding others as better than yourself. What might be a next step in

this collaboration? (Prayers of confession? Conversations with someone? Specific actions?) Explain your response.

Key Terms

Quiet diligence: Persistence, determination, perseverance, endurance, and following God's guidance on when to push through and when to be quiet.

Diligence in forgiveness: The act of forgiving the same offense again and again, no matter what and even if the person is insincere. Jesus wants us to set ourselves up to forgive endlessly.

Diligence in prayer: The act of continuing to pray for our requests and not giving up in our interactions with God. Just engaging with God in conversation will help us not lose heart.

Diligence in humility: The act of completely depending on God. We don't assume that we can "fix" things on our own or through our own strength but instead bring those things to God.

For Further Reading

Kenneth Bailey, *Jesus Through Middle Eastern Eyes: Cultural Studies in the Gospels* (Lisle, IL: InterVarsity Press, 2008), chapter 27.

Klyne Snodgrass, *Stories with Intent: A Comprehensive Guide to the Parables of Jesus* (Grand Rapids, MI: Wm. B. Eerdmans, 2018), chapter 6, about the parables in this chapter.

LESSON 15

MOVED BY COMPASSION

Parable of the Good Samaritan (Luke 10:30–37)

[God] sends us the people to whom we can be a neighbor.

DALLAS WILLARD

The Russian author Leo Tolstoy told a story about a man named Martin, a devout shoemaker who was reading the Bible when it came to him that Jesus would visit him that day. Martin moved expectantly through the morning, working on shoes. He lived in a basement where he could see the feet of the people as they passed by through a window, and so he looked for the feet of the Master. But by noon, Jesus had not come.

As the afternoon wore on, an old soldier friend came in who had no money. They talked, and as he went away, the cobbler gave him a coat to keep him warm because he was freezing on the street. Later on, Martin went to buy some bread for the evening. He found a little child who was lost and took him to his mother.

He then met an old woman on the street who was in need of food, so he took her in and gave her some soup and bread.

As the evening came to a close, Martin said, "Lord, was I wrong? The day is over, and you haven't come." It was then he heard these words: "Whatever you did for one of the least of these brothers and sisters of mine, you did for me" (Matthew 25:40).[1]

The same theme underlies the Parable of the Good Samaritan that we will discuss in this lesson. This parable displays the practical outworking of the "word of the kingdom" that we first studied in the Parable of the Sower back in lesson 3. In the kingdom of God, we love our neighbor. This word, *neighbor,* comes from Middle English and is from a time when the word *boor* or *bur* referred to a citizen who was a peasant. The term *nigh* meant "near," so a neighbor is anyone who is in close proximity to us or standing in front of us.

Our closest neighbors are those who are closely involved in our lives: our family, friends, coworkers. We start there and move outward to the people we meet every day. As the Samaritan in this parable reveals, a stranger can be a neighbor. We make ourselves "present" to that stranger, and when we notice a need in that person that we can meet, we do so.

We can add the Samaritan to the many characters we have studied who were "rich in good deeds" (1 Timothy 6:18), including: the host who invited anybody and everybody to his wedding feast (lesson 5), the vineyard owner who gave his tenants second and third chances to be honest (lesson 8), the father who welcomed both his wild son and his self-righteous son (lesson 9), the king who forgave enormous debts (lesson 11), and the landowner who hired anyone who wanted to work (lesson 12). These individuals in Jesus' stories lived their everyday lives and found a moment to do good, relying on the resources of the kingdom of God.

1. When, if ever, have you had an experience of being surprised by someone helping you when you had not requested assistance? If you have experienced this, how did it make you feel?

2. When have you surprised someone you knew by helping him or her in some way? Or helping someone you *barely* knew? How did that make you feel?

Hearing What Jesus Said

Jesus once found himself in a discussion with a lawyer (an expert in Jewish law) who seemed uneasy with him quoting the Great Commandment (to love God and love one's neighbor) as the way to inherit eternal life. Perhaps this called to mind someone whom the lawyer did not *want* to love. So he asked a more niggling question: "Okay, then, just *who is* my neighbor?" (see Luke 10:25–29). In response, Jesus told him the Parable of the Good Samaritan:

> "A certain man went down from Jerusalem to Jericho, and fell among thieves, who stripped him of his clothing, wounded him, and departed, leaving him half dead. Now by chance a certain priest came down that road. And when he saw him, he passed by on the other side. Likewise a Levite, when he arrived at the place, came and looked, and passed by on the other side" (Luke 10:30–32 NKJV).

The beaten man appears to have been a Jew. According to the Jewish law, he would have qualified as a "neighbor" to the priest and the Levite, so they were *required* to help him. But the priest didn't stop to look, perhaps because he knew that if he looked, he would feel responsible. Perhaps he was afraid of being the next victim or was focused on memorizing Scripture. The Levite *did* look, which makes sense, as the Levites were helpers in the priestly work. The Levite, at least, paused and looked, but like the priest, he also passed by. Perhaps they were worried about being ineligible for service at the temple if they touched a dead body. Jesus didn't reveal their reasons and so was not trying to make them look bad.

> "But a certain Samaritan, as he journeyed, came where he was. And when he saw him, he had compassion. So he went to him and bandaged his wounds, pouring on oil and wine; and he set him on his own animal,

> brought him to an inn, and took care of him. On the next day, when he departed, he took out two denarii, gave them to the innkeeper, and said to him, 'Take care of him; and whatever more you spend, when I come again, I will repay you'" (Luke 10:33–35 NKJV).

Imagine driving down a steep, curving road (like the Jerusalem to Jericho road even today) and seeing a person lying unconscious there. It occurs to you that if this person were conscious, he or she might tell you to stay away because of something about you the person found objectionable—your ethnicity, gender, politics (maybe even something on your bumper sticker!). But this person is *unconscious*, so you are free to help in some way. This was the case with the Samaritan. He seems to have traveled that road regularly enough for the innkeeper to trust him to pay the balance when he returned. He did what was needed in that moment.

3. Put yourself in the place of the Samaritan. What reasons might you have to keep on going like the priest and the Levite did? What reasons might you have to stop and help?

4. What do you admire most about the Samaritan? That he wasn't afraid to stop? His practical, hands-on caring of the wounded man? Or something else? Who has shown you empathy or compassion? (Consider that you are one of *their* treasures in heaven!)

Thinking About What Jesus Said

Compassion for Others

When this "certain Samaritan" came along and looked, he felt compassion ("with passion") for the suffering man. A prerequisite for doing to others as we would have them do to us is to feel how others feel (see Matthew 7:12). This makes love practical. We then have some idea of what *they* would like us to do by thinking about what *we* would like them to do if we were in their place. The primary attribute of that Samaritan was that he could "feel" with other people. He was not so caught up in his plans or goals that he couldn't look at others and help. His compassion was not just about feelings but also about actions. True compassion combines the head and heart but also the hands and feet. The Samaritan looked, felt, and then acted.

Bob Pierce, the founder of World Vision, often prayed, "Let my heart be broken by the things that break the heart of God."[2] Such a prayer helps us identify with others—to take the time to feel with them, to put ourselves in their place, and to imagine how it would be if we were in their place. To share the mind and heart of Christ is to be prepared to feel toward people and situations in the way that Jesus did. The results are that we might cry a great deal more than we do now—or laugh more than we do now.

In the words of the apostle Paul, to feel with other people involves learning to "rejoice with those who rejoice; mourn with those who mourn" (Romans 12:15). Paul was not saying to fake it. Instead, we *enter into* their joy and *enter into* their sorrow. The Samaritan had that ability to enter into these things, which is a gift God can also give us.

We may hesitate and even be frightened at the thought of entering into compassion with others. How could we feel with *every person* who came by? By the end of the day, we might be wiped out! But we would also enjoy a tremendous sense of connection from these experiences. We would have the opportunity to help people feel truly seen and truly heard. Tears and joy are a part of the full dimension of the life that God intends us to live.

5. What are some things in our world today that you think break the heart of God?

6. Choose one of the items that you just listed. Take a moment to think about how a person in that situation might feel (trapped, rejected, stuck, fearful, anxious, physically hurt, emotionally damaged). Write our your thoughts in the space below.

Considering Others Made in God's Image

Sometimes it is difficult to put ourselves in the place of other people, especially when they are not like us or we have had conflicts with them. A great test of our spiritual life is how much we can *feel* with them. Jesus chose one of the Jews' hated enemies, the Samaritans, to be the role model of compassion in his parable. This would have caused an earthquake in the listeners' prevailing cultural beliefs—which makes this the most scandalous parable of all!

The term *Samaritan* was a holdover from the days when the ten northern tribes of Israel intermarried with the people of the land who were not Israelites. They created a religion for themselves that the Jews considered heresy, establishing their center of worship at a temple on Mount Gerizim instead of in the city of Jerusalem. When the Jews returned from captivity to rebuild Jerusalem (as recorded in the books of Ezra and Nehemiah), the Samaritans opposed them. As a result, a proper Jew felt disgust for these people of mixed heritage.

It can be difficult for us to remember that people who are different from us or with whom we've had conflicts are people made in the image of God (see Genesis 1:27). Or perhaps the issue is that we met one person like them (in terms of ethnicity or other traits) whom we found objectionable, and so we cross off the person who needs help along with the entire group. We assume they are all the same, even though we know that people vary widely! In reality, most people are like us—they love their families and work hard to make ends meet. They have the same feelings, virtues, and character. Of course, there are also those who are violent, lazy, and immoral in *every* people group. Every race or ethnicity is a mixed bag!

Jesus truly saw everyone as made in God's image. When we read the Gospels, again and again we see his compassion for people of different social classes and of different racial and cultural backgrounds. Jesus taught the Jews primarily because they were prepared to receive him, but he cared for everyone with whom he came into contact. He had a sense of people's suffering. He knew that the gospel of the kingdom of God was available to *all*.

7. How are people hurt by their distaste for other people just because those individuals are not from their own group (whether that is ethnic, cultural, or otherwise)?

8. Pause for a few minutes and situate yourself in a place of quiet—perhaps outside or looking out a window. Ask God to show you whom you may consider a "Samaritan." It may be an ethnic group, or people in certain professions, or anyone who looks like your mother! Now write down what you think Jesus sees when he looks at that person. Finally, say aloud, "Every person I stand before is 'holy ground' in God's eyes."[3]

Answering the Questioner

Jesus told the Parable of the Good Samaritan after seventy-two of his followers had healed people and cast out demons, acting in the power of the kingdom of God (see Luke 10:1–24). As Jesus celebrated this, the lawyer who was in a position of great authority and power stood by and watched. No doubt he questioned what was happening because he believed that it was people such as himself who would exercise God's power—not ordinary, unschooled men. So he decided to take the offensive and test Jesus by asking what needed to be done to inherit eternal life. Jesus didn't develop arguments but simply asked the lawyer what he already knew.

When it comes to witnessing and teaching, most folks already have an idea about the answers. Sometimes they need something clarified or confirmed or maybe an example set out for them, but basically, they know. People also don't need condemnation and blame. Most people have already condemned *themselves* because they know what they have done wrong. Jesus said, "I did not come into the world to condemn the world" (John 3:17, paraphrase). Of course, now and then there is a need for us to say a tender word about what someone should do. If that is our role, then we need to speak in a spirit of helpfulness and firmness.

In this case, Jesus thought the best way to answer the lawyer was with a story. He included a Samaritan because he was knew how the religion of the Jews had blocked them from loving others. Jesus' response worked better than if he had offered a definition of the word *neighbor* or a list of who the lawyer's neighbors might be. By telling this intriguing story, Jesus helped the lawyer explore the kingdom of God. The story changed the question from "Who is my neighbor?" to "To whom will I be a neighbor?" In truth, the question "Who is my neighbor?" was the wrong one because there was no end to how it could be discussed and debated. The kingdom question is, "To whom will we be a neighbor?"

9. Notice that Jesus didn't blame the lawyer for his question. He just answered him in a way that was disarming (a story) and inspiring (we would all want to be like the Samaritan). What are some wise ways to respond to a questioner? Some unwise ways?

10. Some people are easy to approach with questions. (The lawyer might have understood this was the case with Jesus.) What is it about such people that makes this so?

Responding to What Jesus Said

Interruptions as Holy Moments

The Samaritan allowed himself to be *interrupted* in his routine travel. Like him, our lives consist of many interruptions. These can either defeat us or become opportunities that we will be glad not to miss. More than half of Jesus' healings were interruptions by people who needed healing or by their friends or relatives. He submitted to these interruptions, interacted with the hurting persons, and healed them. He saw where he was needed and took time for people.

Perhaps the priest and the Levite were usually compassionate, but this time they thought, *I don't have time right now. I will get another chance. I will help next time.* When we have this mindset and don't allow ourselves to be interrupted, we miss out on opportunities. Even minor interruptions—like choosing to look up from our monitor when we are interrupted at work to engage in eye contact with the other person—can lead to important opportunities for discussions that we might otherwise miss. At first it may be hard to get into the routine of accepting such disruptions in our day, but over time we will find it becomes a joy.

Loving your neighbor as you love yourself is active and on the go. It is a state of being alert to the fact that those you come across (the ones "nigh" you)—even though you might have never seen them before, and even though they are unlike you—are at that moment your neighbors. In that moment, your question to God should be, *What does this person in my path need from me right now?* Nothing may come to you, but you will be in a state of readiness that will allow you to respond unknowingly but will also allow the Holy Spirit to work easily through you. Neighboring is an opportunity in the kingdom of God.

11. How do you typically deal with interruptions in your day? Are there people to whom you normally pay partial attention and need to turn, face them, smile, and listen intently?

12. Close by writing out a prayer, asking God to help you respond with unselfconscious action the next time you encounter someone in need. (If you need help, consider this reality from 2 Peter 1:3: "His divine power has given us everything we need for a godly life through our knowledge of him who called us by his own glory and goodness.")

Key Term

Neighbor: The word *neighbor* comes from the Middle English *neighebor*, with *nigh* meaning "near" and *boor* or *bur* meaning a citizen who was a peasant. A neighbor is thus anyone who is "near"—someone in close proximity to us or even standing in front of us.

For Further Reading

Dallas Willard, *The Divine Conspiracy: Rediscovering Our Hidden Life in God* (HarperCollins, 1998), chapter 4.

Trevor Hudson, *A Mile in My Shoes: Cultivating Compassion* (Nashville, TN: Upper Room Books, 2005).

Kenneth Bailey, *Jesus Through Middle Eastern Eyes: Cultural Studies in the Gospels* (Lisle, IL: InterVarsity Press, 2008), chapter 22.

David Wenham, *The Parables of Jesus* (Lisle, IL: InterVarsity Press, 1989), chapter 8, about the Parable of the Good Samaritan.

Notes

1. Leo Tolstoy, *Where Love Is There God Is Also* (New York: Thomas Y. Crowell, 1887).
2. Franklin Graham with Jeanette Lockerbie, *Bob Pierce: This One Thing I Do* (Waco, TX: Word Books, 1983), 77.
3. Ronald Rolheiser, *Chastity and the Soul: You Are Holy Ground* (Paraclete Press, 2024), Kindle edition, 5.

ABOUT THE AUTHOR

Dallas Willard (1935–2013), author of *The Scandal of the Kingdom,* was a professor at the University of Southern California's School of Philosophy from 1965 until his retirement in 2012. His groundbreaking books *The Divine Conspiracy, The Great Omission, Knowing Christ Today, The Spirit of the Disciplines, Renovation of the Heart,* and *Hearing God* forever changed the way that thousands of Christians experience their faith. For more information, visit dwillard.org.

Jan Johnson, author of *The Scandal of the Kingdom Workbook,* is a writer, speaker, and spiritual director who has degrees in biblical studies and Christian spirituality. She has written twenty-three books, including *Enjoying the Presence of God* and *When the Soul Listens,* in addition to many magazine articles. She is also a frequent retreat and conference speaker. Jan spends most of her work days writing from her office at her home in Simi Valley, California. For more information, visit her website at JanJohnson.org.